# PRENTICE HALL ②

# Realidades

# Writing, Audio & Video Workbook

PEARSON

Prentice
Hall

Boston, Massachusetts
Upper Saddle River, New Jersey

## Acknowledgments

"Soñando con Puerto Rico" written by Bobby Capo. Used by permission of Edward B. Marks Music Company.

"Campo" from PUERTO RICO, PUERTO RICO, MI TIERRA NATAL. Copyright © 1990 by Shanachie Entertainment Corporation

"En mi viejo San Juan" by Noel Estrada. Music Sales.

"Canción con todos" by César Isella and A. Tejada Gómez. Sociedad Argentina de Autores y Compositores de Musica (SADAIC). Latin Copyrights, Inc.

"Cuento del mundo" by Emma Junaro from EMMA JUNARO; MI CORAZÓN EN LA CIUDAD. Copyright © 1992 by Riverboat Music.

"La media vuelta" by José Antonio Jiménez. BMG Music Publishing Inc.

"Canción mixteca" written by José López Alavés. Copyright © 1929 by Edward B. Marks Music Company, Copyright Renewed. All rights reserved. Used by permission.

"Sólo lo pido a Dios" by Juan Ángel Porillo. Copyright © 1974 by Peer International Corporation. All rights Reserved.

"Verde luz" by Antonio Caban Vale. PeerMusic.

"Mi cuatrito" by Ladislao Martínez from PUERTO RICO, PUERTO RICO, MI TIERRA NATAL. Copyright © 1990 by Shanachie Entertainment Corporation.

"Y volver, volver, volver" by Fernando Z. Maldonado. EMI Music Publishing, Inc.

*Note: Every effort has been made to locate the copyright owner of material used in this textbook. Omission brought to our attention will be corrected in subsequent editions.*

16   09
ISBN 0-13-036008-2

**Realidades 2**

**Para empezar**

Nombre _____

Fecha _____

Hora _____

**AUDIO**

## Actividad 1

As an icebreaker for the first week of school, a teacher asks his students to draw a poster that describes him or her. Listen as each student describes him- or herself and match each description to one of the bio-posters below. Write the corresponding number underneath the poster. You will hear each description twice.

## Actividad 2

As a second-year Spanish student, David is helping in the school counselor's office during the first week of school. As Spanish-speaking students enroll, he asks their name and nationality. Listen to each conversation, then circle the native country of the Spanish-speaking student. You will hear each conversation twice.

1. Bolivia, Chile, Uruguay

2. Argentina, Paraguay, Uruguay

3. Honduras, Panamá, Nicaragua

4. México, Puerto Rico, España

5. El Salvador, República Dominicana, Venezuela

**Realidades 2**

**Para empezar**

Nombre _____

Fecha _____

Hora _____

**AUDIO**

## Actividad 3

After Alicia enrolls at the counselor's office, David offers to show her to her first class. As he walks her to class, he points out his friends to her and tells her what each is doing. Match the pictures with each description of his friends. You will hear each description twice.

A.

B.

C.

D.

E.

1. _____ 2. _____ 3. _____ 4. _____ 5. _____

## Actividad 4

Look at the people pictured. Choose two adjectives from the box to describe each person or group of people and write them on the blanks provided. You may use each adjective more than once. Don't forget to change the adjective endings as necessary!

| | | |
|---|---|---|
| alto | guapo | paciente |
| atrevido | impaciente | reservado |
| bajo | inteligente | serio |
| deportista | joven | sociable |
| estudioso | ordenado | trabajador |
| gracioso | viejo | |

1. _____ _____

2. _____ _____

3. _____ _____

4. _____ _____

5. _____ _____

6. _____ _____

**Realidades 2**

**Para empezar**

Nombre _____

Fecha _____

Hora _____

**WRITING**

## Actividad 5

Read the descriptions of the new students below and then write a complete sentence to describe each of them. Use at least three different adjectives in each sentence.

1. Marisol trabaja con niños que tienen mucha energía. Ella tiene 24 años y tiene muchos amigos.

   _____

   _____

2. Gabriel tiene 29 años y es profesor de italiano. Él estudia mucho y trabaja 12 horas al día. También corre mucho y le encanta montar en bicicleta.

   _____

   _____

3. Juanita y Nicolita son amigas. Ellas hablan por teléfono todas las noches. Las dos tienen el pelo bonito y largo, y estudiaron en universidades muy buenas de Boston.

   _____

   _____

4. A David y a Linda les gusta jugar al tenis todas las semanas. También trabajan mucho en la casa y en el jardín. Les gusta pintar y tocar el piano.

   _____

   _____

5. ¿Cómo eres tú?

   _____

   _____

**Realidades** 2

**Para empezar**

Nombre _____

Hora _____

Fecha _____

**WRITING**

## Actividad 6

Some students at school are talking about the things they and their families do on the weekends. Look at each sequence of pictures and tell what the subject does, using the present tense.

**1.** Ramiro _____

_____

**2.** Mi familia y yo _____

_____

**3.** Yo _____

_____

**4.** Patricia y Chucho _____

_____

**Realidades 2**

**Capítulo 1A**

Nombre _____

Fecha _____

Hora _____

**VIDEO**

# Antes de ver el video

## Actividad 1

Imagine that you are a teacher and it is your first day of classes. Write four expressions you might use to address the class. The first one is done for you.

*¡Buenos días!* _____

_____

_____

_____

# ¿Comprendes?

## Actividad 2

In the video, Esteban dreams he is a teacher. Circle the best choice to complete the sentences or answer the questions about his dream below.

1.  En el video, Esteban es el profesor de

    a. matemáticas.

    b. español.

    c. ciencias sociales.

    d. historia.

2.  ¿A qué hora empieza la clase de Esteban?

    a. a las diez y cinco

    b. a las nueve y seis

    c. a las nueve y cinco

    d. a las once y seis

**Realidades 2**

**Capítulo 1A**

Nombre _____

Fecha _____

Hora _____

**VIDEO**

3. En la clase de historia Esteban piensa dar un discurso sobre

   a. los verbos regulares en el presente.

   b. cómo hay que prestar atención al profesor.

   c. los presidentes de los Estados Unidos.

   d. la vida de George Washington.

4. Angélica y Lisa tienen que quedarse en la escuela después de las clases porque

   a. no tienen los libros.

   b. llegan tarde a la clase.

   c. hacen demasiadas preguntas.

   d. no saben qué hora es.

5. ¿Cuál *no* es una regla de la clase de Esteban?

   a. Los estudiantes tienen que estar en sus asientos cuando empieza la clase.

   b. Hay que respetar a los demás.

   c. Todos necesitan ir al armario.

   d. Hay que prestar atención al profesor.

**Realidades 2**

**Capítulo 1A**

Nombre _____

Hora _____

Fecha _____

**VIDEO**

## Actividad 3

Identify the speaker of each of the following quotes from the video.

1. Mamá, ¿por qué estás aquí en la clase? _____

2. ¡Esteban! ¿Qué te pasa? _____

3. Señoritas, ¿saben qué hora es? _____

4. ¿Hay tarea esta noche? _____

5. ¿Por qué estás delante de la clase? _____

6. Lo siento. Pero se prohíbe ir al armario. _____

7. ¿A qué hora llegas a casa después de las clases? _____

8. Esteban, ¿qué es esto? ¿Tú eres profesor? _____

9. Soy el profesor Ríos. _____

10. ¿Qué pasa? ¿Dónde estoy...? _____

# Y, ¿qué más?

## Actividad 4

All teachers have rules for their students. We already know Esteban's rules. Imagine that you are Esteban and write three more rules for your class.

_____

_____

_____

**Realidades** ❷

**Capítulo 1A**

Nombre _____

Hora _____

Fecha _____

**AUDIO**

## Actividad 5

Listen to these teachers welcoming their students to the first day of class. The pictures below correspond to things that the students must and cannot do in their classes. In the boxes under each teacher's name, write the letters of the pictures that correspond to what you must and cannot do in his or her class. There should only be one letter per box. You will hear each set of statements twice.

A.    B.    C.    D.

E.    F.    G.    H.

I.    J.

| | Srta. Arcos | Sr. Cruz | Sra. Cazón | Sra. Rendón | Srta. García |
|---|---|---|---|---|---|
| **No se permite** | | | | | |
| **Hay que** | | | | | |

**Realidades** ❷

**Capítulo 1A**

Nombre _____

Fecha _____

Hora _____

**AUDIO**

## Actividad 6

Listen as students talk about their classes this semester. Decide which class each one is describing and write the name of the class in the grid below. Then, place a check mark in the box below the class name if the student likes the class, and an X if the student doesn't like the class. You will hear each set of statements twice.

| | 1 | 2 | 3 | 4 | 5 |
|---|---|---|---|---|---|
| **Clase** | | | | | |
| **¿Le gusta (✓) o no le gusta (x)?** | | | | | |

## Actividad 7

Teachers and students all talk about their classes with their friends and family. Listen to snippets of their conversations to see if you can determine whether it is a teacher or a student who is talking about his or her classes. Write an X in the appropriate box in the grid. You will hear each set of statements twice.

| | 1 | 2 | 3 | 4 | 5 | 6 |
|---|---|---|---|---|---|---|
| **Profesor(a)** | | | | | | |
| **Estudiante** | | | | | | |

**Realidades** 2

**Capítulo 1A**

Nombre _____

Hora _____

Fecha _____

**AUDIO**

## Actividad 8

After listening to each of the following statements about school, decide whether it is **lógico** or **ilógico** and mark your answer on the grid. You will hear each statement twice. At the end of the exercise, you may want to compare your answers with those of a partner.

|          | 1 | 2 | 3 | 4 | 5 | 6 | 7 | 8 | 9 | 10 |
|----------|---|---|---|---|---|---|---|---|---|----|
| **Lógico**  |   |   |   |   |   |   |   |   |   |    |
| **Ilógico** |   |   |   |   |   |   |   |   |   |    |

## Actividad 9

Listen as a reporter for the teen magazine *¿Qué hay?* talks to students about their "secrets" for doing well in school. Fill in the grid below with their secret for each category: 1) **La cosa más importante para sacar buenas notas** (*the most important factor in getting good grades*); 2) **El mejor lugar para estudiar** (*the best place to study*); 3) **Si es mejor estudiar solo(a) o con amigos** (*whether it's better to study alone or with friends*). You will hear each set of statements twice.

|                                                    | 1 | 2 | 3 | 4 |
|----------------------------------------------------|---|---|---|---|
| **La cosa más importante para sacar buenas notas** |   |   |   |   |
| No tener televisor en el dormitorio                |   |   |   |   |
| Buena organización                                 |   |   |   |   |
| Dormir ocho horas                                  |   |   |   |   |
| Tener un profesor paciente que explica todo        |   |   |   |   |
| **El mejor lugar para estudiar**                   |   |   |   |   |
| La cocina                                          |   |   |   |   |
| La biblioteca                                      |   |   |   |   |
| El dormitorio                                      |   |   |   |   |
| La sala                                            |   |   |   |   |
| **¿Solo(a) o con amigos?**                         |   |   |   |   |
| Solo(a)                                            |   |   |   |   |
| Con amigos                                         |   |   |   |   |

**Realidades** ②

**Capítulo 1A**

Nombre _____

Fecha _____

Hora _____

**WRITING**

## Actividad 10

Things are busy at school today. Look at the scene and write five complete sentences that describe what the people indicated are doing. One has been done for you.

| Modelo | *Manuel hace una pregunta.* |

1. _____

_____

2. _____

_____

3. _____

_____

4. _____

_____

5. _____

_____

## Actividad 11 ·

Look at the pictures below and write two complete sentences to tell about what's happening in each one. Then, write one complete sentence that describes your experience or opinion about the activity indicated. Follow the model.

**Modelo**

_Los trabajadores de la cafetería sirven la comida_ ___

_Los estudiantes prefieren comer pizza_ .

_Yo almuerzo a las once y media de la mañana_ .

1. _____
   _____
   _____

2. _____
   _____
   _____

3. _____
   _____
   _____

4. _____
   _____
   _____

5. _____
   _____
   _____

## Actividad 12

You are completing a survey about your life at school. Look at each of the statements in the survey. If you agree with the statement, put an X by it and write an explanation. If you disagree with the statement, rewrite it on the lines below, changing it to make it true for you and your experiences at school. Follow the model.

**Modelo**      __X__   Hay muchas escuelas con más reglas que nuestra escuela.

*Hay algunas escuelas que tienen menos reglas, pero nuestra escuela*
*puede tener más.*

_____ **1.** No conozco a nadie en mi escuela.

_____

_____

_____

_____ **2.** Nunca tenemos tarea los fines de semana.

_____

_____

_____

_____ **3.** Siempre prestamos atención en la clase.

_____

_____

_____

_____ **4.** Todos los estudiantes sacan buenas notas.

_____

_____

_____

_____ **5.** En la clase de español hacemos un proyecto cada semana.

_____

_____

_____

_____ **6.** La comida de la cafetería siempre es buena.

_____

_____

_____

Nombre _____    Hora _____

Fecha _____

## Actividad 13

**A.** Look at the picture below of Universidad Troyana. Based on the picture, circle the activities in the bank that people do there.

| leer | estudiar | repetir | dormir |
|------|----------|---------|--------|
| bailar | almorzar | pedir | poder |
| jugar | esquiar | servir | cocinar |

**B.** Now, using the verbs above, complete the ad below that some students are writing to attract people to the Universidad Troyana.

*¡La Universidad Troyana es la mejor! Aquí, nosotros...*

- _____ .
- _____ .
- _____ .
- _____ .

Para aprender más sobre nuestra universidad, lee lo que dice una de nuestras estudiantes:

*"¡Hola! Yo soy Catalina, una estudiante de primer año aquí en la Universidad Troyana. Me encanta la vida aquí. Todos los días yo...*

- _____ .
- _____ .
- _____ .
- _____ .

*Realmente es la mejor universidad."*

Nombre _____     Hora _____

Fecha _____     **VIDEO**

# Antes de ver el video

## Actividad 1

What extracurricular activities are there in your high school? When does each activity take place? Name at least five activities in your school and their schedules. Follow the model.

| Actividades extracurriculares | El horario |
|---|---|
| club de español | De las tres y media a las cuatro y media de la tarde, todos los lunes |
|  |  |
|  |  |
|  |  |
|  |  |
|  |  |

# ¿Comprendes?

## Actividad 2

Put the following scenes in the order in which they occur in the video. Write **1** under the first scene and **7** under the last scene.

_____     _____     _____     _____

_____     _____     _____

Nombre _____ Hora _____

Fecha _____

**VIDEO**

## Actividad 3

Read the following descriptions of the students in the video. Then, write the name of the student being described in the space provided.

1. Es miembro del club de computadoras. _____

2. Trabaja después de las clases. _____

3. Le encanta el primer día de clases. _____

4. Es miembro del coro y de la orquesta. _____

5. Es deportista. _____

6. Es talentosa. _____

7. Tiene computadora portátil. _____

8. Según Lisa es misterioso. _____

9. Toma lecciones de artes marciales en un club atlético. _____

10. Quiere ser miembro del equipo de natación en el invierno. _____

## Y, ¿qué más?

## Actividad 4

Look again at the six extracurricular activities from **Actividad 1**. Survey your class to find out how many students participate in each activity. Then, record your findings in the table below. The first one is done for you.

| Actividades extracurriculares | ¿Cuántos estudiantes? |
|---|---|
| club de español | Hay seis muchachos en el club de español. |
| | |
| | |
| | |
| | |
| | |

Nombre _____   Hora _____

Fecha _____   **AUDIO**

## Actividad 5

As part of freshman orientation, students can go to the **Feria de clubes** to find the perfect club or activity for them. Write the number of the conversation next to the name of the corresponding club or activity that is being discussed by the two people. You will hear each conversation twice.

El club de ajedrez _____          El club de arte _____

El club de artes marciales _____   El coro _____

El club de baile _____            El club de fotografía _____

La orquesta _____                 El club de computadoras _____

## Actividad 6

What do Lorena and her friends do after school? Listen to the conversations they are having at lunch and place the number of each conversation in the grid under the corresponding picture. You will hear each conversation twice.

_____   _____   _____   _____

_____   _____   _____   _____

## Actividad 7

Although they are best friends, Ana and Elisa are very competitive with each other. Listen as each girl tries to convince the other that her boyfriend (**novio**) is as wonderful as the other girl's boyfriend! Write the letter of the picture that corresponds to each part of the conversation. You will hear each part of the conversation twice.

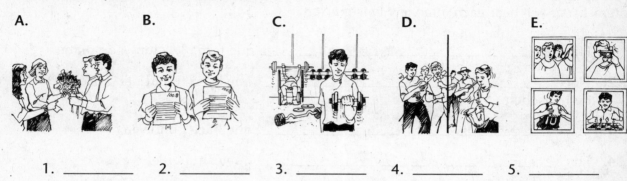

A.          B.          C.          D.          E.

1. _____  2. _____  3. _____  4. _____  5. _____

## Actividad 8

Javier's Mom does not know all of her son's friends by name, but she is familiar with what each one knows how to do well. Listen as she asks Javier about each of them. Match Javier's answers to the pictures below and write the name of his friend next to the picture. You will hear each conversation twice.

## Actividad 9

We all know the expression "practice makes perfect." Listen as high school seniors are interviewed by a Hispanic radio station about the scholarships (**becas**) they received for their outstanding achievements in their extracurricular activities. Complete each sentence by writing the amount of time each of them has been involved with his or her particular interest. You will hear each interview twice.

1.  Hace _____ que toma lecciones de piano.

2.  Hace _____ que escribe para el periódico de la escuela.

3.  Hace _____ que hace gimnasia.

4.  Hace _____ que canta en el coro.

5.  Hace _____ que participa en las artes marciales.

6.  Hace _____ que crea páginas Web.

7.  Hace _____ que toca el violín en la orquesta.

Nombre _____

Hora _____

Fecha _____

**WRITING**

## Actividad 10

It's time to submit biographies for the school yearbook. Answer the questions below based on the pictures, writing a complete sentence in response to each question.

**1.** ¿De qué club es miembro Rosa?

_____

_____

¿A qué ensayo necesita asistir esta tarde?

_____

_____

**2.** ¿A qué juegan Marcos y Jorge?

_____

_____

¿En qué deporte participa Jorge también?  ¿Y Marcos?

_____

_____

**3.** ¿Qué deporte le gusta a Mariela?

_____

_____

¿Qué más le gusta hacer?

_____

_____

**4.** ¿Y tú? ¿En qué deportes o clubes participas?

_____

_____

¿Qué te gusta hacer?

_____

_____

**Realidades** ②

**Capítulo 1B**

Nombre _____

Fecha _____

Hora _____

**WRITING**

## Actividad 11

You are comparing all of the after-school clubs that you are thinking about joining. Look at their fliers below and write sentences comparing the clubs to each other. The first one has been done for you.

| **CLUB DE ESPAÑOL** | **CLUB DE FOTOGRAFÍA** | **CLUB DE AJEDREZ** |
|---|---|---|
| *Hay:* | *Hay:* | *Hay:* |
| –27 miembros | –16 miembros | –16 miembros |
| –20 reuniones al año | –14 reuniones al año | –20 reuniones al año |
| –más de 8 actividades al año | –8 actividades cada año | –8 actividades cada año |
| *Es:* | *Es:* | *Es:* |
| –un club educativo | –un club recreativo | –un club recreativo |
| –un club para todos | –un club para todos | –sólo para personas inteligentes |
| *Cuesta:* | *Cuesta:* | *Cuesta:* |
| –12 dólares al año | –20 dólares al año | –12 dólares al año |

1. *El club de ajedrez es tan popular como el club de fotografía.* _____

2. _____

3. _____

4. _____

5. _____

6. _____

7. _____

**Realidades 2**

**Capítulo 1B**

Nombre _____

Hora _____

Fecha _____

**WRITING**

## Actividad 12

Imagine that you are preparing questions for a Spanish-language game show. You are given topics and must produce two logical and gramatically correct questions about each topic: one using the present tense of the verb **saber** and one using the present tense of the verb **conocer**. Use the model to help you write your questions.

**Modelo**   el alfabeto

¿_Sabes las letras del alfabeto en español_____?

¿_Conoces el alfabeto español_____?

**1.** Madrid

¿_____?

¿_____?

**2.** el ajedrez

¿_____?

¿_____?

**3.** la natación

¿_____?

¿_____?

**4.** el libro *Don Quijote de la Mancha*

¿_____?

¿_____?

**5.** la música latina

¿_____?

¿_____?

**6.** la fotografía

¿_____?

¿_____?

**7.** las reglas de tu escuela

¿_____?

¿_____?

Nombre _____     Hora _____

Fecha _____     **WRITING**

## Actividad 13

**A.** Imagine that you are preparing to interview the busiest student in your school, Alfonso, to find out how long he has been participating in all of his activities. Below is a list of things he does during the week. Write the six questions you are going to ask him. Follow the model.

soy miembro del club de ajedrez

hago gimnasia

ensayo con la orquesta

asisto a las reuniones del club de fotografía

participo en la natación

tomo lecciones de artes marciales

juego a los bolos

| Modelo | *¿Cuánto tiempo hace que juegas a los bolos?* |

1. ¿_____?

2. ¿_____?

3. ¿_____?

4. ¿_____?

5. ¿_____?

6. ¿_____?

**B.** Now, write a paragraph about at least three activities you participate in and say how long you have been doing each of them. Supply at least two additional details about each activity. Follow the model.

| Modelo | *Hace tres años que juego a los bolos. Juego con mi papá los sábados y siempre gano.* |

_____

_____

_____

_____

_____

_____

_____

Nombre _____ Hora _____

Fecha _____

VIDEO

# Antes de ver el video

## Actividad 1

What do you do every morning? In the table below, write at least five activities you do each day. One has been done for you.

| Por la mañana... |
|---|
| *Me despierto.* |
| |
| |
| |
| |
| |

# ¿Comprendes?

## Actividad 2

Decide whether each statement about the video is **cierto** or **falso.** If a statement is false, rewrite it to make it true.

1. _____ Raúl y Tomás están muy interesados en el programa de televisión.

_____

2. Gloria recibe una llamada de teléfono.

_____

3. Raúl y Tomás quieren participar en una obra de teatro.

_____

4. Hay una emergencia en el teatro y Gloria necesita la ayuda de tres personas mañana.

_____

**Realidades 2**

**Capítulo 2A**

Nombre _____

Fecha _____

Hora _____

**VIDEO**

5. Tomás piensa que la experiencia puede ser interesante.

_____

6. Tomás se ve mal.

_____

7. Raúl tiene que lavarse la cara, cepillarse los dientes, ponerse desodorante y vestirse.

_____

8. Los muchachos tienen cincuenta minutos para prepararse.

_____

# Actividad 3

Write the appropriate word or words in the spaces provided.

1. Raúl no se quiere poner tanto _____.

2. Tomás pregunta: ¿Es necesario _____ los labios?

3. La señora de maquillaje pide _____ y _____.

4. Esto fue idea de _____.

5. Tomás le dice a Raúl que la ropa de payaso (*clown*) no es muy _____.

**Realidades 2**

**Capítulo 2A**

Nombre _____

Hora _____

Fecha _____

**AUDIO**

## Actividad 7

Listen as a young model and her photographer describe a typical weekend photo shoot to a magazine reporter. They will mention specific activities that they do at particular times during the day. Write the time of day that the reporter and the model say that they do each thing. Be careful! Not all of the squares will be filled for both people. You will hear this dialogue twice.

| | La modelo | El fotógrafo |
|---|---|---|
| | 6:00 A.M. | |
| | | |
| | | |
| | | |
| | | |
| | | |
| | | |
| | | |
| | | |
| | | |
| | | |

Nombre _____

Fecha _____

Hora _____

**AUDIO**

## Actividad 8

Parents are sometimes surprised to learn from teachers that their children act differently at school than they do at home. Listen to mothers, who are volunteering in the school today, as they talk to their children's teachers. How do the mothers view their children? According to the teachers, how are they acting today in class? Fill in the chart below with adjectives as you listen. You will hear each dialogue twice.

|  | Ana | Javier | Laura | Mateo | Linda | Joaquín |
|---|---|---|---|---|---|---|
| **Según la madre, ¿cómo es su hijo(a)?** |  |  |  |  |  |  |
| **Según el (la) profesor(a), ¿cómo está su hijo en clase?** |  |  |  |  |  |  |

## Actividad 9

Listen as Claudia's father tries to sort out all of the items left at their home after his daughter's friend Laura spent the night. As you listen to the conversation, sort out which items belong to Claudia and which belong to Laura. Under each picture, write the first initial of the person the item belongs to. You will hear this conversation twice.

_____

_____

_____

_____

_____

_____

_____

_____

**Realidades** 2

**Capítulo 2A**

Nombre _____

Fecha _____

Hora _____

**WRITING**

## Actividad 10

Write complete sentences to tell what the following people have to do each morning and what items they use while doing these activities. Follow the model.

Pancho

Teresa and Lolis

Juanita

Alicia

Cristina

Raúl

Yo

| Modelo | *Pancho no tiene que arreglarse el pelo* _____ |

1. _____

2. _____

3. _____

4. _____

5. _____

6. _____

**Realidades 2**

**Capítulo 2A**

Nombre

Fecha

Hora

**WRITING**

## Actividad 11

Esteban is never able to get to school on time. Describe what he does each morning, using the pictures to guide you. **¡OJO!** Some of the verbs are reflexive, while others are not. The first one has been done for you.

*Primero, Esteban se levanta.*

_____

_____

_____

_____

_____

_____

_____

**Realidades 2**

**Capítulo 2A**

Nombre _____

Hora _____

Fecha _____

**WRITING**

## Actividad 12

The people below are on vacation. First, complete the questions about them and their trips by circling the correct verbs. Then, answer the questions in complete sentences.

1.  ¿Dónde (es, está) Lola?

    _____

2.  ¿De dónde (es, está)?

    _____

3.  ¿Cómo (es, está) ella hoy? ¿Contenta?

    _____

4.  ¿Cómo (es, está) ella? ¿Baja?

    _____

5.  ¿Qué (es, está) haciendo en este momento?

    _____

6.  ¿Dónde (son, están) los señores Obregón?

    _____

7.  ¿De dónde (son, están)?

    _____

8.  ¿Cómo (son, están)? ¿Perezosos?

    _____

9.  ¿Cómo (son, están) hoy? ¿Tristes?

    _____

10. ¿Qué (son, están) haciendo en este momento?

    _____

**Realidades 2**

**Capítulo 2A**

Nombre _____

Hora _____

Fecha _____

**WRITING**

## Actividad 13

**A.** Think of the items you and your family members use every day. Which things are yours, which are theirs, and which are common to everyone in the family? Make a list of three items in each column.

| Mine | My family members' | Ours |
|------|--------------------|------|
| _____ | _____ | _____ |
| _____ | _____ | _____ |
| _____ | _____ | _____ |

**B.** Now, write a descriptive paragraph about what you and your family members do with each of these items. Follow the model.

Modelo   *Yo me arreglo el pelo todos los días con el gel mío.*

_____

_____

_____

_____

_____

_____

_____

_____

_____

_____

_____

_____

_____

_____

Nombre _____ Hora _____

Fecha _____

**VIDEO**
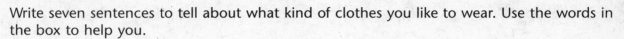

# Antes de ver el video

## Actividad 1

Write seven sentences to tell about what kind of clothes you like to wear. Use the words in the box to help you.

| | | | | |
|---|---|---|---|---|
| la ganga | la liquidación | el mercado | algodón | de cuero |
| está hecho(a) de | claro(a) | oscuro(a) | vivo(a) | apretado(a) |
| flojo(a) | mediano(a) | la talla | el dinero | el regalo |
| el precio | los pantalones | la blusa | la falda | la chaqueta |
| tela sintética | | | | |

1. _____

2. _____

3. _____

4. _____

5. _____

6. _____

7. _____

# ¿Comprendes?

## Actividad 2

Circle the correct response below.

1.  Gloria ve un letrero que

   **a.** anuncia una liquidación fabulosa.

   **b.** informa al público de una tienda nueva.

   **c.** tiene el horario de la tienda favorita de Gloria.

2.  A Raúl y a Tomás no les gusta

   **a.** ir al mercado.

   **b.** ir de compras.

   **c.** tomar refrescos.

**Realidades 2**

**Capítulo 2B**

Nombre _____

Fecha _____

Hora _____

**VIDEO**

**3.**  Gloria compró una blusa que era

   **a.** de talla extra-grande.

   **b.** muy fea.

   **c.** una ganga.

**4.**  Tomás quiere ir

   **a.** a casa.

   **b.** al centro comercial.

   **c.** al mercado.

**5.**  Gloria exclama: "Aquellas blusas tienen

   **a.** un estilo muy bonito."

   **b.** unos colores aburridos."

   **c.** muchas tallas, pero ninguna me sirve."

**6.** A Gloria le gusta la blusa

   **a.** un poco floja.

   **b.** bien apretada.

   **c.** de cuero.

**7.** La blusa está hecha de

   **a.** lana.

   **b.** algodón.

   **c.** seda.

**8.** Gloria dice que

   **a.** Raúl es muy impaciente.

   **b.** Raúl es su hermano favorito.

   **c.** Raúl no se viste de moda.

**9.** Raúl

   **a.** tiene dinero para gastar, aunque le dijo a Gloria que no tenía nada.

   **b.** no tiene nada de dinero.

   **c.** le pide prestado dinero a Gloria.

**10.**  Gloria paga por su blusa

   **a.** con cheque.

   **b.** en efectivo.

   **c.** con tarjeta de crédito.

**VIDEO**

## Actividad 3

Match each character with three things he or she said in the video. Write the number of the statement next to the corresponding name.

**El personaje**

Gloria _____ _____ _____

Tomás _____ _____ _____

Raúl _____ _____ _____

**Lo que dice**

1. ¡Una liquidación fabulosa! ¿Qué les parece?

2. Bueno, no me importa, pero creo que los precios son muy altos.

3. ¿Hay un mercado cerca de aquí?

4. … por favor, ¿otra blusa?

5. Me queda un poco floja. Pero me gusta así…

6. ¿De qué está hecha?

7. ¿El precio? A ver… 9,400 colones.

8. Mira. Aquellas chaquetas de cuero.

9. Pero no tienes dinero.

## Y, ¿qué más?

## Actividad 4

Do you like to shop? Write a short paragraph telling why or why not.

**Modelo** *A mí no me gusta mucho ir de compras. A mi hermana, sin embargo, le encanta comprar de todo. Por eso no me gusta salir con ella. Pero cuando quiero comprar discos compactos, vamos al centro comercial. Yo voy a las tiendas de discos y ella va a las de ropa. Ella gasta todo su dinero y yo no gasto mucho. Lo mejor de todo es que al final puedo comprarme un helado.*

_____

_____

_____

_____

_____

_____

## Actividad 5

Listen to a group of friends as they shop in the popular Madrid department store **El Corte Inglés**. As you listen, figure out which of the factors below is most important to each of them when deciding what to buy. Some may have more than one answer. Put an X in the appropriate column(s) for each girl. You will hear this conversation twice.

| | El precio | La moda/ El estilo | La marca | La talla/cómo te queda(n) |
|---|---|---|---|---|
| Alicia | | | | |
| Marta | | | | |
| Carmen | | | | |
| Luz | | | | |
| Lorena | | | | |

## Actividad 6

Some people enjoy shopping, while others find it frustrating. Listen to several conversations as people look for particular items in a department store. Match the conversations to the pictures by writing the number of the conversation it represents under each picture. You will hear each conversation twice.

_____    _____    _____

_____    _____    _____

Nombre _____

Hora _____

Fecha _____

**AUDIO**

## Actividad 7

Listen to the following teenagers describe to a radio announcer the most daring thing they have ever done. As the radio interviewer asks each one "**¿Cuál es la cosa más atrevida que hiciste?**", look at the pictures below. Write the number of each response under the corresponding picture. You will hear each response twice.

_____

_____

_____

_____

_____

_____

Nombre _____

Hora _____

Fecha _____

## Actividad 8

This semester, Eleanor is hosting an exchange student from Ecuador named Marta. Listen as they talk about different items in a department store. Based on each description, place an X on the line labeled A or B to indicate which one accurately represents what is said in each conversation. You will hear each conversation twice.

1.

      A. _____        B. _____

2.

      A. _____        B. _____

3.

      A. _____        B. _____

4.

      A. _____        B. _____

Nombre _____

Hora _____

Fecha _____

**AUDIO**

## Actividad 9

Listen as Mariana shops for several gifts for her friends as well as a few things for herself. In each department she is able to narrow her choices down to two, and then finally makes her selection. In the spaces below, check off all the items that she decides to buy. You will hear each conversation twice.

1. 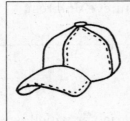   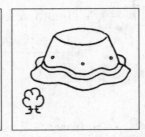   2.

_____     _____

3.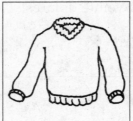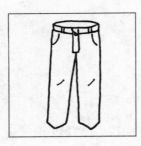

_____

4.    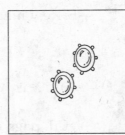   5.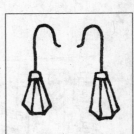

_____     _____

**Realidades** 2

**Capítulo 2B**

Nombre _____

Fecha _____

Hora _____

**WRITING**

## Actividad 10

There is a sale at your local department store this weekend and you've run into many of your friends there, shopping for bargains. Complete the mini-conversations below.

—¡Aquellos zapatos cuestan sólo veinte dólares!

—¿Cómo sabes que son tan baratos?

**Modelo**

— _El letrero anuncia la liquidación_ _____.

—¿De qué color es el suéter que tienes en la mano?

— _____.

—¿Y cuesta sólo nueve dólares?

1. —Sí, _____.

—Señor, me gustaría ver aquellos zapatos.

—Claro, señorita. ¿_____?

2. —Siete y medio.

—¿Ud. paga con cheque personal?

3. —No, _____.

—Ramón, tengo unas camisas en colores pastel para ti.

4. —Gracias, papá, pero _____.

**Realidades 2**

**Capítulo 2B**

Nombre _____

Hora _____

Fecha _____

**WRITING**

## Actividad 11

Write complete sentences to tell what the following people did yesterday. Use the correct preterite form of the verbs suggested by the pictures. Follow the model and be creative.

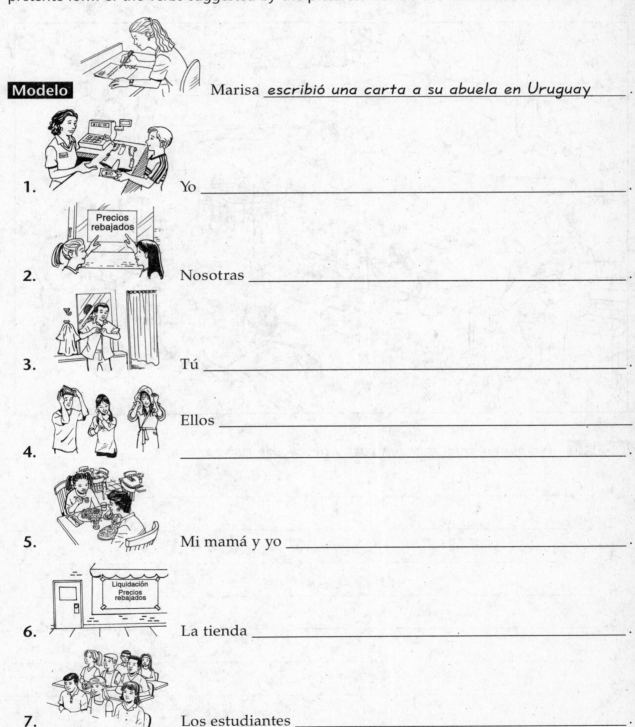

**Modelo**    Marisa *escribió una carta a su abuela en Uruguay* _____.

1. Yo _____.

2. Nosotras _____.

3. Tú _____.

4. Ellos _____
   _____.

5. Mi mamá y yo _____.

6. La tienda _____.

7. Los estudiantes _____.

Nombre _____ Hora _____

Fecha _____

WRITING

## Actividad 12

Alicia is thinking about the things she sees around her in the park. Describe these items in relation to her in the picture using a form of **este, ese,** or **aquel.** Follow the model.

**Modelo**   *No tengo calor porque estoy debajo de este árbol.*

1. _____

2. _____

3. _____

4. _____

5. _____

6. _____

7. _____

Nombre _____    Hora _____

Fecha _____

**WRITING**

## Actividad 13

Imagine that the items of clothing below are yours.  Describe each item and tell when you wore it last. Follow the model.

**Modelo**

*Aquellos pantalones son diferentes. Llevé estos jeans cuando pinté la casa hace una semana. Llevé los grises a la escuela ayer.*

1. _____

_____

_____

_____

2. _____

_____

_____

_____

3. _____

_____

_____

_____

Nombre _____ Hora _____

Fecha _____

**VIDEO**

# Antes de ver el video
## Actividad 1

Following is a list of things that the characters from the video did during the day. In the second column, write the place where they probably went to do each thing. The first one has been done for you.

| Cosas que hacer | Lugar |
|---|---|
| *ir a ver una película* | *el cine* |
| 1. comprar champú y pasta dental | |
| 2. llenar el tanque de gasolina | |
| 3. enviar una carta | |
| 4. comprar unos patines | |
| 5. comprar un regalo | |
| 6. comprar sellos | |

# ¿Comprendes?
## Actividad 2

First, match each statement on the right with its corresponding picture, using the letters **a-e**. Then, number the scenes in each section in the order in which they occur in the video. Write **1** for the first scene and **5** for the last. One is done for you.

**A. Teresa y Claudia**

a.

b.

c.

_____*b*_____ Claudia habló con Ramón por el celular para ir al Bazar San Ángel. ___5___

_____ Teresa escoge el champú que va a comprar. _____

_____ Teresa fue al correo para comprar sellos. _____

Nombre _____ Hora _____

Fecha _____

**VIDEO**

d. _____ Teresa y Claudia se encontraron. _____

e. _____ Teresa necesita comprar varias cosas en la farmacia. _____

**B. Ramón y Manolo**

a. _____ El asistente llenó el tanque. _____

b. _____ Manolo y Ramón fueron a la estación de servicio para llenar el tanque de gasolina. _____

c. _____ Manolo y Ramón fueron a la tienda de deportes, porque querían saber cuánto costaban los patines. _____

d. _____ Ramón habló con Claudia por el celular para ir al Bazar San Ángel. _____

e. _____ Ramón se compró una camiseta del Cruz Azul. _____

**Realidades 2**

**Capítulo 3A**

Nombre _____

Hora _____

Fecha _____

**VIDEO**

## Actividad 3

Circle the correct word that completes the following sentences.

1. Los cuatro amigos quieren ir al (cine/correo) a ver una película (romántica/ de ciencia ficción).

2. Teresa no compró el champú (ayer/hoy), porque fue a (devolver/comprar) un libro a la biblioteca.

3. (Claudia/Teresa) compra pasta dental en la farmacia.

4. El correo (abre/cierra) a las cinco.

5. A Teresa se le olvidó (llenar el tanque/enviar la carta) esta mañana.

6. Manolo (compra/no compra) los patines en la tienda de equipo deportivo.

7. Teresa olvidó (enviar/comprar) un regalo para el cumpleaños de su (abuela/mamá).

8. Claudia y Teresa van a ver a Ramón y a Manolo en el (correo/Bazar San Ángel) porque (no está muy lejos/ está muy lejos) de allí.

# Y, ¿qué más?

## Actividad 4

Write four complete sentences that tell about things you and your friends do and places that you and your friends go to in your free time. Follow the model.

**Modelo**   *Me gusta ir con mis amigos(as) a jugar a los bolos.*

_____

_____

_____

_____

**Realidades** 2

**Capítulo 3A**

Nombre _____

Hora _____

Fecha _____

**AUDIO**

## Actividad 5

Miguel is calling his friends to make plans for the day, but no one is available. Listen as each friend tells Miguel what he or she is doing, then write his or her name in the space under the picture that best illustrates the activity. You will hear each conversation twice.

**Realidades 2**

**Capítulo 3A**

Nombre _____

Hora _____

Fecha _____

**AUDIO**

## Actividad 6

Felipe has been trying to catch up with his friend Moisés all day. As he asks people where they saw Moisés last, write the time and place each person mentions on the line beneath the appropriate picture. After you have heard everyone's answers, number the pictures chronologically, with **1** being the first place Moisés went and **8** being the last place Moisés went. You will hear each conversation twice.

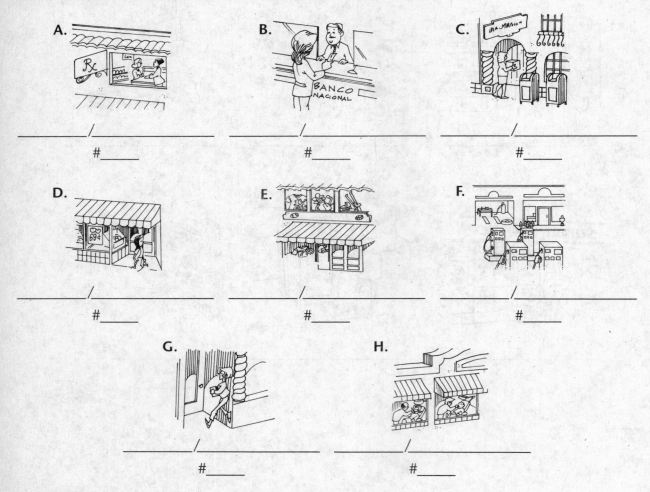

A. _____/_____
#_____

B. _____/_____
#_____

C. _____/_____
#_____

D. _____/_____
#_____

E. _____/_____
#_____

F. _____/_____
#_____

G. _____/_____
#_____

H. _____/_____
#_____

## Actividad 7

Listen as you hear several people describe a moment when they saw someone who they thought was good-looking. After each statement, complete the sentence below with the correct location of the encounter. You will hear each statement twice.

**1.** Lo vio en _____

**2.** La vio en _____

**3.** Los vio en _____

**4.** Las vio en _____

**5.** La vio en _____

## Actividad 8

When Eric went to Mexico for the summer, he brought his high school yearbook with him so that his host family could see what his school was like. Listen as his host parents look through his yearbook and reminisce about their own high school days. They will ask each other if they remember (**¿recuerdas?**) certain events from their past. Match their memories with the corresponding pictures. You will hear this conversation twice.

_____  _____  _____

_____  _____

## Actividad 9

Sometimes there just aren't enough hours in the day! Listen as each person tells a friend what he or she had to do yesterday but just wasn't able to. As you listen to each conversation, fill in the grid below with short phrases. You will hear each conversation twice.

| | ¿Qué tuvo que hacer la persona? | ¿Por qué no pudo hacerlo? |
|---|---|---|
| 1. | | |
| 2. | | |
| 3. | | |
| 4. | | |
| 5. | | |

**WRITING**

# Actividad 10

Write complete sentences telling where these people have to go today in order to accomplish the tasks depicted in the drawings.

**1.** Marta

_____

_____

**2.** Tito

_____

_____

**3.** Marisa y Laura

_____

_____

**4.** Juanito

_____

_____

**Realidades 2**

**Capítulo 3A**

Nombre _____

Hora _____

Fecha _____

**WRITING**

## Actividad 11

Your little sister is curious about some of the things you have in your room. Explain what each item is, what you use it for, and when you use it, using complete sentences. Follow the model.

**Modelo** _Son periódicos. Los leo todos los días después de terminar la tarea._

1. _____

2. _____

3. _____

4. _____

5. _____

6. _____

7. _____

**Realidades 2**

**Capítulo 3A**

Nombre _____

Hora _____

Fecha _____

**WRITING**

## Actividad 12

You witnessed a bank robbery last night! Look at the pictures below that illustrate what happened, then write complete sentences to answer the police officer's questions that follow. Use the preterite forms of the verbs **ser** and/or **ir** in each sentence.

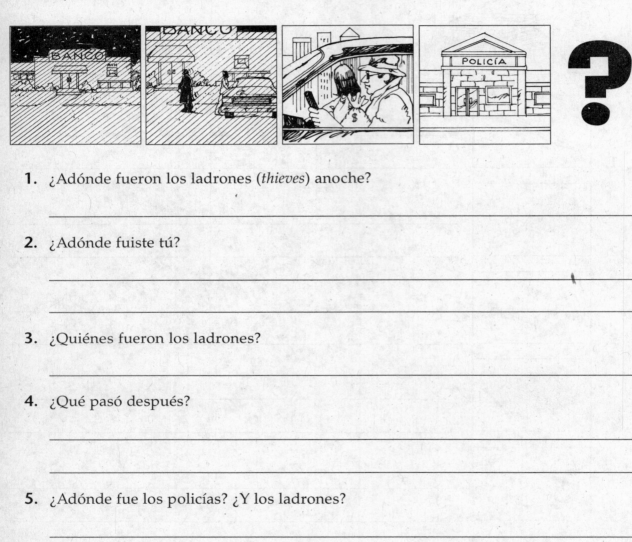

**1.** ¿Adónde fueron los ladrones (*thieves*) anoche?

_____

**2.** ¿Adónde fuiste tú?

_____

_____

**3.** ¿Quiénes fueron los ladrones?

_____

**4.** ¿Qué pasó después?

_____

_____

**5.** ¿Adónde fue los policías? ¿Y los ladrones?

_____

_____

Nombre _____ Hora _____

Fecha _____

**WRITING**

## Actividad 13

Your family just took a trip and you are going through your photos, reminiscing about the good and bad parts of the vacation. Write a caption for each picture below to describe what everyone did, where they went, what they were able to do there, etc.

**Modelo**

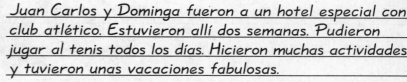

*Juan Carlos y Dominga fueron a un hotel especial con club atlético. Estuvieron allí dos semanas. Pudieron jugar al tenis todos los días. Hicieron muchas actividades y tuvieron unas vacaciones fabulosas.*

1. _____
_____
_____
_____

2. _____
_____
_____
_____

3. _____
_____
_____

Nombre _____   Hora _____

Fecha _____

# Antes de ver el video

## Actividad 1

How do you get to your Spanish classroom from the cafeteria? Write the directions on the lines below.

_____

_____

_____

_____

_____

# ¿Comprendes?

## Actividad 2

Who made each comment or asked each question below? Write the name of the corresponding character from the video in the space provided.

1. Vamos a tomar el metro. _____

2. Mira, aquí hay un banco… ¿Tienes prisa? _____

3. Hace mucho tiempo que no voy por allí. Pero te va a gustar.

   _____

4. ¿Estás seguro que sabes cómo llegar? _____

Nombre _____ Hora _____

Fecha _____

**VIDEO**

5. Espera… Esto es complicado. _____

6. Claro, claro. Me estás poniendo nervioso. Yo sé por dónde vamos.
_____

7. Ya son las dos y cuarto. ¿Dónde estarán…? _____

8. ¡Basta! Vamos a preguntar a alguien. _____

9. Oye, ¿podemos caminar un poco más despacio? _____

10. Mira. Allí está el bazar. _____

Nombre _____ Hora _____

Fecha _____

**VIDEO**

# Actividad 3

Manolo and Ramón want to meet up with Teresa and Claudia. Answer the questions below about the events that take place along the way.

**1.** ¿Cómo van Manolo y Ramón al Bazar San Ángel? ¿Y cómo llegan Claudia y Teresa allí?

_____

_____

**2.** ¿Quién llega al bazar primero? ¿Qué hacen allí?

_____

_____

**3.** ¿A cuántas personas pregunta Ramón sobre cómo se va al Bazar San Ángel?

_____

_____

# Y, ¿qué más?

## Actividad 4

You want to tell your friend how to get to the local YMCA, since she wants to play basketball. Use the following expressions to write directions.

doblas a (la derecha / la izquierda)

sigues (la avenida *nombre* / la calle *nombre*)

hasta (el primero / el segundo / el próximo) semáforo

sigues derecho por (esa avenida / esa calle) aproximadamente (dos / tres / cinco) millas

sigues esa avenida por (seis / siete / ocho) cuadras, hasta que veas el gimnasio

_____

_____

_____

_____

Estaciona el coche, y ¡a jugar al básquetbol!

Nombre _____   Hora _____

Fecha _____

## Actividad 5

Listen as people in a hotel call the front desk for help. As you listen to each conversation, match each caller to the spot on the map below by writing the number of the conversation in the corresponding circle. You will hear each conversation twice.

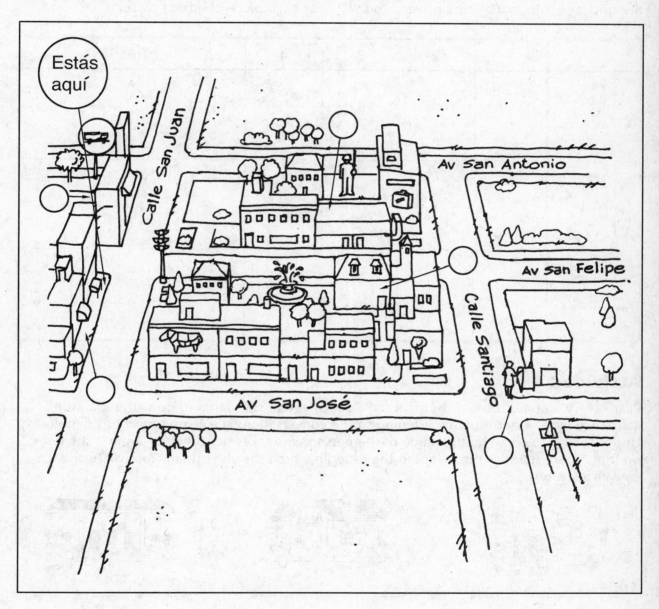

**Realidades 2**

**Capítulo 3B**

Nombre _____

Fecha _____

Hora _____

**AUDIO**

# Actividad 6

Parents always seem to worry about their children as soon as they step out the door! As you listen to the parent's last piece of advice as each young person leaves, determine whether the young person is walking, riding a bicycle, or driving a car to his or her destination. Use the grid below to mark your answers. You will hear each piece of advice twice.

|  | 1 | 2 | 3 | 4 | 5 | 6 | 7 |
|---|---|---|---|---|---|---|---|
|  |  |  |  |  |  |  |  |
|  |  |  |  |  |  |  |  |
|  |  |  |  |  |  |  |  |

# Actividad 7

Pilar is very ambitious today, but she can't get to where she wants to go without a little assistance. Follow her route by listening to the conversations she has with various people. Under each picture, write the name of the person who takes her there, or **a pie** if she goes on foot. Then, number the places in the order in which she visits them. You will hear each conversation twice.

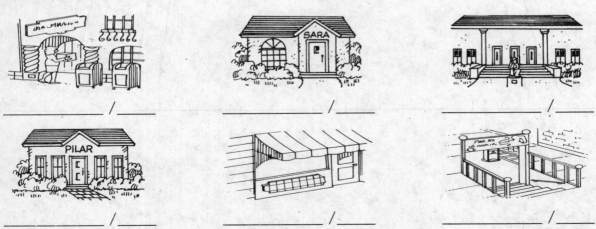

_____ / _____    _____ / _____    _____ / _____

_____ / _____    _____ / _____    _____ / _____

Nombre _____  Hora _____

Fecha _____

**AUDIO**

## Actividad 8

Listen as an elementary school teacher gives instructions to several of her students during a field trip to a local park. Match each command to a picture of one of the children. In the blanks below, write in the letter of the corresponding picture. You will hear each set of instructions twice.

A.

B.

C.

D.

E.

F.

G.

H.

I.

J.

1. _____    3. _____    5. _____    7. _____    9. _____

2. _____    4. _____    6. _____    8. _____    10. _____

Nombre _____

Fecha _____

Hora _____

**AUDIO**

## Actividad 9

The teacher in charge of after-school detention is going to be absent for a few days. Listen as she describes the students to the substitute teacher. Write the name of each student in the blank under the corresponding picture. You will hear each description twice.

_____   _____   _____   _____

_____   _____   _____   _____

**Realidades 2**

**Capítulo 3B**

Nombre _____

Fecha _____

Hora _____

**WRITING**

## Actividad 10

You are giving directions to some friends about how to get to your cousin's house for a surprise party. Using the map below, tell them what landmarks they will pass on the way from each of their houses to the party.

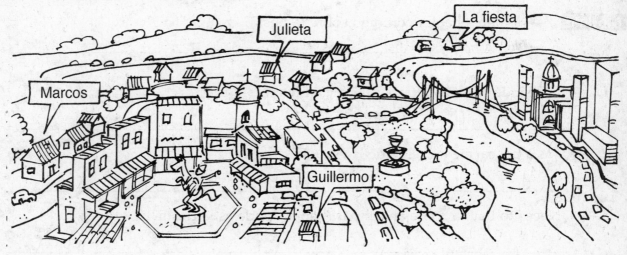

1. Guillermo  _Para llegar a la fiesta, vas a pasar por..._ _____

_____

_____

_____

_____

2. Julieta  _Para llegar a la fiesta, vas a pasar por..._ _____

_____

_____

_____

_____

3. Marcos  _Para llegar a la fiesta, vas a pasar por..._ _____

_____

_____

_____

**WRITING**

## Actividad 11

Your friends rely on you for help with various things. Write out your responses to the questions your friends ask you. You may answer in the affirmative or negative. Follow the model.

**Modelo**  —¿Quieres hablar conmigo sobre la fiesta?

  —*No, te hablé anoche* _____.

1.  —¿En dónde vas a esperar a María y a Elena?

  —_____.

2.  —¿Vas a buscarme enfrente de la escuela?

  —_____.

3.  —¿Necesito llamar a Alejandro para saber dónde es la fiesta?

  —_____.

4.  —¿Alejandro nos invitó a ti y a mí a la fiesta?

  —_____.

5.  —¿Tengo que traer algo a la fiesta para ti?

  —_____.

6.  —¿Necesitas ayuda con algo?

  —_____.

7.  —¿Vienen tus tíos a la fiesta contigo?

  —_____.

8.  —¿Hablaste con ellos anoche?

  —_____.

9.  —¿Quieres ver a alguien en la fiesta?

  —_____.

10.  —¿Conoces a la familia Rodríguez?

  —_____.

**Realidades 2**

**Capítulo 3B**

Nombre _____

Hora _____

Fecha _____

**WRITING**

## Actividad 12

As part of the interview process to become a camp counselor, you are asked to describe to the head counselor what you would tell kids to do in certain situations. Look at each drawing and write two affirmative **tú** commands for each, based on the hints provided. Include at least one of the following verbs each time: **poner, tener, decir, salir, venir, descansar, jugar, quedarse, hacer, ir,** and **ser.**

ve una serpiente (*snake*)

1. _____

_____

acaba de comer

2. _____

_____

no quiere participar

3. _____

_____

está enferma

4. _____

_____

tiene frío

5. _____

_____

no quiere hacer sus quehaceres

6. _____

_____

**Realidades** **2**

**Capítulo 3B**

Nombre _____

Hora _____

Fecha _____

**WRITING**

## Actividad 13

You are keeping a journal of things that happen throughout the day. Look at each picture, and write a complete sentence to tell what time it is and what the people are doing at the moment.   Follow the model.

Modelo _____ Pablo

_Son las dos y diez y Pablo está pidiéndole ayuda a la profesora_ .

1. _____ **Mónica**

_____ .

2. _____ **Jorge**

_____ .

3. _____ **Yo**

_____ .

Sigue, dobla,...

4. _____ **Nosotros**

_____ .

5. _____ **Tú**

_____ .

6. _____ **La señora Vargas**

_____ .

Nombre _____ Hora _____

Fecha _____

**VIDEO**

# Antes de ver el video

## Actividad 1

What were you like when you were younger? Think of several words that describe you. Then, use them in sentences about yourself. One has been done for you.

| Palabras descriptivas | Oración sobre mí |
|---|---|
| generoso(a) | Era muy generoso(a) con mis hermanos pequeños. |
| | Era |
| | Era |
| | Era |

# ¿Comprendes?

## Actividad 2

Do you remember the conversations from the video about Ana as a little girl? Fill in the blanks below with the words that describe Ana in each of the scenes shown.

1. ¿Cómo era Ana de niña?

   Era muy _____.

2. ¿Qué dice Ignacio de Ana?

   Ignacio dice que era _____.

Según su mamá, ¿Ana era _____ de niña?

No, por lo general era muy _____ y muy bien

3. _____.

4. ¿Ana era siempre bien educada de niña?

   No, a veces era un poquito _____.

**VIDEO**

## Actividad 3

All of the following sentences contain incorrect information. Rewrite each sentence to match what you learned in the video.

1. Ana, Elena e Ignacio trabajan en un proyecto para la clase de matemáticas.

_____

2. De niña, Ana no tenía un juguete favorito.

_____

3. Ana solamente tenía un animal de peluche, su oso.

_____

4. De niña, Ana siempre se levantaba tarde.

_____

5. Elena cree que Ignacio siempre obedecía a sus padres y que siempre decía la verdad.

_____

**Realidades 2**

**Capítulo 4A**

Nombre _____

Hora _____

Fecha _____

**VIDEO**

# Y, ¿qué más?

## Actividad 4

Draw a family tree of your immediate family. Next to each person, write a word to describe him or her. Then, write three sentences about your favorite relatives.

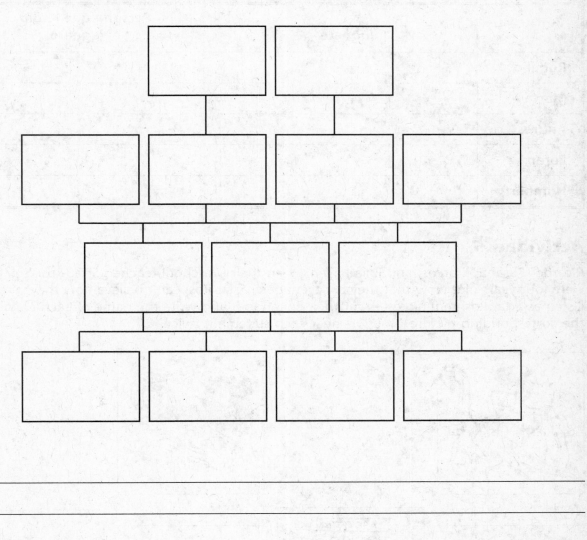

_____

_____

_____

Nombre _____

Hora _____

Fecha _____

**AUDIO**

# Actividad 5

Do you remember your favorite childhood toy? Listen as each of the following people describes a favorite childhood toy. In the grid below, write what each person's favorite toy was and who gave the toy to him or her. You will hear each set of statements twice.

| | Juguete | Persona que le dio el juguete |
|---|---|---|
| **Rogelio** | | |
| **Marta** | | |
| **Andrés** | | |
| **Lorena** | | |
| **Humberto** | | |

# Actividad 6

Ricardo, Susana, Marcos, and Julia haven't seen their preschool teacher, Srta. Rosi, since they were four years old. Now that they are teenagers, Srta. Rosi can't believe how they've grown. Listen as Srta. Rosi reminisces about their childhood, and write the name of each child under the corresponding picture. You will hear each statement twice.

_____

_____

_____

_____

**Realidades 2**

**Capítulo 4A**

Nombre _____

Fecha _____

Hora _____

**AUDIO**

## Actividad 7

Listen as Patricia listens to her favorite popular radio show **"Yo no lo sabía"** to find out things that she didn't know about some of her favorite movie and TV personalities. Match what you hear the DJ say about her favorite celebrities to the pictures below. Write the number of each piece of gossip underneath the picture it refers to. You will hear each piece of gossip twice.

_____

_____

_____

_____

_____

_____

_____

_____

Nombre _____  Hora _____

Fecha _____

**AUDIO**

## Actividad 8

Listen as adults recall their childhood and how they used to role-play having different kinds of jobs when they grew up. Write the number of each description under the picture of the corresponding profession each person imagined as a child. You will hear each description twice.

_____     _____     _____

_____     _____     _____

**Realidades 2**

**Capítulo 4A**

Nombre _____

Fecha _____

Hora _____

**AUDIO**

## Actividad 9

There are no gift tags on the Christmas gifts that the Rodríguez family received from their friend Gonzalo. Sr. Rodríguez has to call him on the phone to find out which gift goes to whom. Complete the sentences below to describe what Gonzalo gave to each person. For example, you might write, "**Gonzalo _le_ dio unos aretes a _la abuela_.**" You will hear this conversation twice.

1. Gonzalo _____ dio unos boletos de avión a _____.

2. Gonzalo _____ dio su colección de tarjetas de béisbol a _____.

3. Gonzalo _____ dio dinero en efectivo a _____.

4. Gonzalo _____ dio unos zapatos de golf a _____.

5. Gonzalo _____ dio una colección de monedas al _____.

## Actividad 10

Look at the scenes of children playing at a day care center. Then, write a sentence to tell what each child is doing.

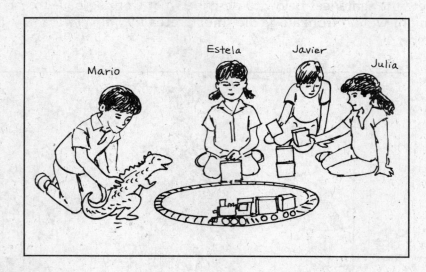

**1.** Mario _____.

**2.** Estela _____.

**3.** Javier y Julia _____.

**4.** Ricardo _____.

**5.** Sandra y Beto _____.

**6.** Susana _____.

**Realidades** ②

**Capítulo 4A**

Nombre _____

Fecha _____

Hora _____

**WRITING**

## Actividad 11

You are at your best friend's family reunion, and all of the relatives are reminiscing about their childhood. Look at the pictures and tell what everyone did as children. Follow the model.

**Modelo**   ¿Qué hacía el abuelito?

*El abuelito pescaba con su padre* _____

1.   ¿Qué hacía la tía Ramona?

_____

2.   ¿Qué hacía el padre?

_____

3.   ¿Qué hacían tú y tu abuela?

_____

4.   ¿Qué hacían los tíos?

_____

5.   ¿Qué hacía la abuela?

_____

6.   ¿Y tú? ¿Qué hacías de niño?

_____

**Realidades 2**

**Capítulo 4A**

Nombre _____

Hora _____

Fecha _____

**WRITING**

## Actividad 12

Read the sentences that tell what the people below used to do when they were your age.
Then, answer the questions that follow in complete sentences. Follow the model.

**Modelo**  Cuando Juliana y María tenían 14 años, ellas contaban muchos chistes *(jokes)*.
Se reían mucho y les gustaba ver las comedias en el cine.

¿Cómo eran las chicas? *Ellas eran cómicas* _____ .

¿Adónde iban para ver las comedias? *Iban al cine* _____ .

1. Cuando Marta tenía 16 años, ella trabajaba mucho. Estudiaba y leía.  También le
   gustaba ver programas educativos en la tele todos los días.

   ¿Cómo era Marta? _____ .

   ¿Qué veía todos los días? _____

   _____ .

2. Cuando Óscar y Humberto tenían 14 años, practicaban muchos deportes. En el
   invierno practicaban el hockey en la calle y en la primavera jugaban al básquetbol
   en el gimnasio.

   ¿Cómo eran los chicos? _____ .

   ¿Adónde iban para practicar sus deportes? _____

   _____ .

3. Cuando nosotros teníamos 15 años, nos gustaba pintar y dibujar. También nos
   encantaba mirar obras de arte de artistas famosos como Dalí y Picasso en el museo.

   ¿Cómo éramos? _____ .

   ¿Adónde íbamos y qué veíamos allí? _____

   _____ .

4. ¿Y tú? ¿Qué hacías cuando eras niño(a)? ¿Cómo eras? ¿Adónde ibas? ¿Qué veías allí?

   _____

   _____

   _____

   _____ .

**Realidades 2**

**Capítulo 4A**

Nombre _____

Hora _____

Fecha _____

**WRITING**

## Actividad 13

**A.** Look at each drawing of people giving gifts to each other. Write a complete sentence to describe what people gave each other. Follow the model.

Los abuelos / Antonio

**Modelo**    *Los abuelos le dieron osos de peluche a Antonio.* _____

La Srta. Rodrigo / Beatriz y Tomás

1. _____

_____

Los padres / Marianela

2. _____

_____

Sebastián y Sergio / Diana y Carmen

3. _____

_____

Elena / Eduardo

4. _____

**B.** Now, tell what presents you and your family members give each other on holidays. Use the present tense and remember to use the appropriate indirect object pronouns.

_____

_____

_____

_____

Nombre _____ Hora _____

Fecha _____

# Antes de ver el video

## Actividad 1

Do you have a favorite holiday or celebration? What is it? Why? Name three special things about it. Follow the model.

**Modelo**     Mi día favorito es *el Día de los tres Reyes Magos.*

*Los Reyes Magos nos traen muchos regalos. Comemos cosas ricas ese día. La familia se reúne a celebrar.*

Mi día favorito es _____

_____

_____

_____

# ¿Comprendes?

## Actividad 2

In a letter, Javier explains his plans for the weekend to a friend, but he has left out certain details. Help him by writing the missing words in the blanks. Use the pictures to help you.

27 de junio

Estimado Salvador,

Este fin de semana me voy con mi amigo Ignacio al pueblo de su madre,

_____. Ignacio me dice que siempre llueve y necesitamos llevar un

paraguas. Durante el fin de semana, ellos celebran la _____.

De niño, él siempre pasaba los veranos allá. Todos los años, la fiesta comienza con un

_____. Hay bailes y músicos, y ellos tocan instrumentos _____

**Realidades 2**

**Capítulo 4B**

Nombre _____

Fecha _____

Hora _____

**VIDEO**

y _____. Algunos de los instrumentos son el txistu y el tamboril.

El txistu es una palabra vasca para una _____. Ignacio sabe tocar el txistu,

pero no sabe hablar _____ , como sus _____. Luego todos se

reúnen en la iglesia, donde celebran una misa en español y en vasco. Esto es una

_____. Bueno, Salvador, te cuento más al regresar.

Tu amigo, *Javier*

## Actividad 3

Match each word or phrase on the left with its corresponding sentence on the right.

1. _____ la fiesta de San Pedro

2. _____ txistu

3. _____ txistorra

4. _____ ropa típica

5. _____ una boina

6. _____ vasco

7. _____ desfile

8. _____ antiguos

9. _____ paraguas

**a.** En la maleta pongo una camisa blanca, un pañuelo rojo y una boina roja.

**b.** Comienza en la mañana, cuando todos nos reunimos en esta marcha ordenada, generalmente para celebrar la fiesta.

**c.** Mi abuelo me enseñó a tocar este instrumento cuando yo era pequeño.

**d.** Este idioma lo hablan los abuelos de Ignacio.

**e.** Me llevo esto para la lluvia porque siempre llueve, pero no importa.

**f.** Los músicos tocan instrumentos típicos y muy viejos, o _____.

**g.** Javier no tiene una gorra redonda, o un tipo de sombrero típico.

**h.** Tienen hambre, y quieren comer este tipo de salchicha.

**i.** Esta fiesta siempre se celebra el 29 de junio.

VIDEO

# Y, ¿qué más?

## Actividad 4

Your cousin invited you this past weekend to spend it with his/her family, for a special celebration. Where did you go and what did you do? In a simple paragraph, explain your weekend. Use your imagination and follow the model.

**Modelo**   *El fin de semana pasado fui a la casa de mi primo favorito, para celebrar su cumpleaños. La fiesta fue en un centro comercial. Allí jugamos a los bolos. Luego comimos un pastel de chocolate y bebimos refrescos. También cantamos y bailamos mucho. Finalmente, regresamos a su casa y dormí allá. Al día siguiente, mis padres volvieron por mí.*

_____

_____

_____

_____

_____

_____

_____

_____

_____

## Actividad 5

Mrs. Lena is taking her third grade class to visit a group of senior citizens tomorrow. In order to make sure that all the children behave well at the Senior Center, she uses puppets named **Marco el malo** and **Bruno el bueno** to illustrate good and bad manners. Listen as she describes what each puppet does, and decide if the actions are most likely those of **Marco el malo** or **Bruno el bueno.** Put an X in the appropriate box in the grid below. You will hear this conversation twice.

| | 1 | 2 | 3 | 4 | 5 | 6 | 7 | 8 |
|---|---|---|---|---|---|---|---|---|
| | | | | | | | | |
| | | | | | | | | |

## Actividad 6

Listen as four people talk about their favorite time to spend with their families. Write the number of the description under the corresponding picture. You will hear each description twice.

_____     _____

_____     _____

Nombre _____

Hora _____

Fecha _____

**AUDIO**

# Actividad 7

When José Ignacio's mother returned from grocery shopping, she was shocked by some of the things her children and their friends were doing! Listen as she later tells José Ignacio's father what was going on when she got home. Based on what she says, fill in the grid below to tell how they were behaving. You will hear each set of statements twice.

|  | 1 | 2 | 3 | 4 | 5 | 6 |
|---|---|---|---|---|---|---|
| **Se portaban bien** |  |  |  |  |  |  |
| **Se portaban mal** |  |  |  |  |  |  |

# Actividad 8

Some best friends like to do everything together, while others prefer to spend some time apart. Listen as some teenagers talk about whether they prefer to do certain things separately or together. Then, put an X in the appropriate box in the grid. You will hear each set of statements twice.

|  | 1 | 2 | 3 | 4 | 5 | 6 | 7 |
|---|---|---|---|---|---|---|---|
| **Juntos** (*together*) |  |  |  |  |  |  |  |
| **Solo** |  |  |  |  |  |  |  |

**Realidades** ❷

**Capítulo 4B**

Nombre _____

Hora _____

Fecha _____

**AUDIO**

## Actividad 9

Listen as parents tell their children about their childhood memories of family celebrations and traditions. As you listen, match each conversation to the pictures below by writing the number of the conversation under the appropriate picture. You will hear each conversation twice.

_____    _____    _____

_____    _____

**Realidades** ❷

**Capítulo 4B**

Nombre _____

Hora _____

Fecha _____

**WRITING**

## Actividad 10

Josephine is an exchange student in Spain and wants to make sure she acts appropriately when greeting people. Help her by answering her questions about what people tend to do in the situations she describes. Follow the model.

**Modelo**  ¿Qué hago para saludar a una persona que conozco bien?

*Uds. se besan o se abrazan para saludarse.*

1. ¿Qué hago cuando encuentro a una persona que no veo con frecuencia?

   _____

   _____

2. ¿Qué digo cuando una persona se casa o se gradúa de la universidad?

   _____

   _____

3. ¿Qué hago cuando conozco a una persona por primera vez?

   _____

   _____

4. ¿Qué hago cuando salgo de un lugar o de la casa por la mañana?

   _____

   _____

5. ¿Qué hago cuando no veo a una amiga por mucho tiempo y quiero verla?

   _____

   _____

6. ¿Qué hago cuando paso a una persona a quien no conozco en la calle?

   _____

   _____

**Realidades 2**

**Capítulo 4B**

Nombre _____

Hora _____

Fecha _____

**WRITING**

## Actividad 11

Your friends had a very eventful weekend. Look at the illustrations of what happened, and write a brief description of what the people in the scene were doing and what happened to interrupt them. Follow the model.

Mónica: *Hacía buen tiempo y Mónica estaba en el parque. Corría cuando empezó a llover.*

1.

Pancho y Patricia: _____

2.

Nosotras: _____

_____

3.

Ellos: _____

_____

4.

Yo: _____

_____

**Realidades 2**

**Capítulo 4B**

Nombre _____

Fecha _____

Hora _____

**WRITING**

## Actividad 12

**A.** Lolis and Teresa are cousins who live quite far away from each other. Look at the pictures below and write complete sentences about what they do. Follow the model.

Modelo _Las primas se quieren mucho y se llevan muy bien._

1. _____

2. _____

_____

3. _____

_____

4. _____

_____

5. _____

_____

**B.** Now, write about a cousin or other relative you like who lives far away. Follow the model.

Modelo _Mi prima Cristina y yo nos vemos una vez cada dos años._

_____

_____

Nombre _____    Hora _____

Fecha _____

**WRITING**

## Actividad 13

Pablo's family has just returned from a family reunion and he is writing in his diary about the day's events.

**A.** First, look at the picture of the party and write several sentences to describe the scene.

_____

_____

_____

_____

**B.** Next, tell what everyone at the party did when they were first reunited.

_____

_____

_____

_____

**C.** Finally, help Pablo write his diary entry using the phrases that you wrote above and any connecting words you may need to make your paragraph smooth.

*Querido diario:*

*Hoy fui a la reunión de mi familia en San Juan.* _____

_____

_____

_____

_____

_____

_____

**Realidades** 2

**Capítulo 5A**

Nombre _____

Hora _____

Fecha _____

**VIDEO**

# Antes de ver el video

## Actividad 1

In this video, you are going to see part of a television newscast. Fill out the survey below about the news program that you normally watch at home.

Nombre del noticiero _____

Canal _____

Horario _____

¿Recuerdas el nombre de algún reportero (alguna reportera)? _____

_____

¿Te gusta más ver los deportes? ¿las noticias? ¿el pronóstico del tiempo (*weather forecast*)?

¿Por qué te gusta esa sección más? _____

_____

# ¿Comprendes?

## Actividad 2

Read the following parts of the plot. Then, put them in the order in which they occurred. Write **1** for the first thing that happened and **7** for the last thing that happened.

_____ Raúl y Tomás ven el noticiero en la tele.

_____ Raúl y Tomás hablan con la reportera.

_____ Comienza el incendio.

_____ Ocurre la explosión.

_____ El bombero habla con la reportera.

_____ Un vecino ve el humo.

_____ Vienen los paramédicos.

## Actividad 3

In the video, Raúl and Tomás are watching TV when they hear the news about a fire. What happens afterwards? Answer the following questions in order to better understand the plot.

**1.** ¿En dónde ocurre el incendio?

_____

**2.** ¿Quién es Laura Martínez? ¿Por qué está en el sitio del incendio?

_____

_____

**3.** ¿Cómo comenzó el incendio?

_____

**4.** ¿Quién estaba en la casa cuando ocurrió el incendio?

_____

**5.** ¿Quiénes vinieron para ayudar a rescatarlos?

_____

**6.** ¿Por qué la reportera termina rápido la entrevista con Raúl y Tomás?

_____

_____

Nombre _____  Hora _____

Fecha _____

**VIDEO**

# Y, ¿qué más?

## Actividad 4

Imagine that you are a reporter for a television newscast and you have to report on something that happened in your high school. Write a reporting script about a real or imaginary event at your high school. Follow the model.

**Modelo**  *Les habla Lucía Pacheco, del canal 8. Estamos en el colegio Spring, donde un grupo de estudiantes de noveno grado está lavando coches. El dinero que reciben es para pagar un viaje a San Antonio, organizado por la profesora de historia, la Sra. Martínez. El viaje está planeado para el próximo mes de marzo. Esto es todo por ahora. Lucía Pacheco, desde el colegio Spring, para el canal 8.*

_____

_____

_____

_____

_____

_____

_____

Nombre _____   Hora _____

Fecha _____

## Actividad 5

Listen as these radio announcers break into regular programming to report emergency situations that have occurred. Match each radio report with one of the pictures below to indicate what type of emergency or crisis situation each was. Then, try to answer the bonus question in the last column for each news report. You will hear each report twice.

| | | | | | | Bonus Question |
|---|---|---|---|---|---|---|
| **1** | | | | | | Según sus vecinos, ¿qué es el Sr. Morales? _____ |
| **2** | | | | | | ¿Qué fue(ron) destruido(s)? _____ |
| **3** | | | | | | ¿Qué necesita la gente? _____ |
| **4** | | | | | | ¿Cómo puede ir la gente de un lugar a otro? _____ |
| **5** | | | | | | ¿Quién es Gabriel? _____ |

**Realidades** ②

**Capítulo 5A**

Nombre _____

Hora _____

Fecha _____

**AUDIO**

## Actividad 6

As Ernesto is driving home from work, he turns on the radio and starts to scan for his favorite type of music. Each time he finds a station, a reporter is in the middle of the evening news report. As you listen, write the number of the excerpt under the corresponding picture. You will hear each report twice.

## Actividad 7

A local jewelry store manager is holding a contest for young couples who purchase their wedding rings in his store. If there is bad weather on their wedding day, the manager promises to refund the couple the cost of their rings! Listen as each couple describes their wedding day. Which couples would qualify for a refund? Mark your answers in the grid below. You will hear each description twice.

|  | 1 | 2 | 3 | 4 | 5 | 6 |
|---|---|---|---|---|---|---|
| **Qualify** |  |  |  |  |  |  |
| **Do not qualify** |  |  |  |  |  |  |

**Realidades 2**

**Capítulo 5A**

Nombre _____

Hora _____

Fecha _____

**AUDIO**

## Actividad 8

When it comes to the news, some people prefer to listen to the radio while others would rather read the newspaper. Listen to people talk about recent events. Determine whether they HEARD about it on the radio or if they READ about it in the newspaper. Place a check mark in the appropriate row of the grid.  You will hear each conversation twice.

|  | 1 | 2 | 3 | 4 | 5 |
|---|---|---|---|---|---|
| |  |  |  |  |  |
| |  |  |  |  |  |

## Actividad 9

Your teacher has asked you to listen to the news on a Spanish-speaking radio station. First, read the questions below. Then, listen to a news report of a hurricane that occurred yesterday in a small town near San Juan. As you listen to the story, circle the correct answers below. Your teacher might ask you to write a summary of the news story based on your answers. You will hear the report twice.

1. ¿Quién es Carmen Dominó?

   a. Una reportera.    b. Una bombera.    c. Una heroína.

2. ¿Qué es Felipe?

   a. Un noticiero.    b. Un huracán.    c. Un pueblo.

3. ¿Qué hacían muchas personas cuando el huracán llegó?

   a. Escuchaban la radio.    b. Leían.    c. Dormían.

4. ¿Qué pasó en Dorado a causa del huracán?

   a. Había mucha comida.    b. Muchos vecinos perdieron sus casas.

   c. Había muchos muebles.

5. ¿Quiénes fueron los héroes de Dorado?

   a. Los médicos.    b. Los reporteros.    c. Los bomberos.

**Realidades 2**

**Capítulo 5A**

Nombre _____

Fecha _____

Hora _____

**WRITING**

## Actividad 10

You just finished watching the evening news. Under each news category below, write a short summary of the stories of the day by looking at each picture and using appropriate vocabulary. The first one has been started for you.

1.  El tiempo

_Hoy pasó un gran huracán por las islas de Venezuela._

_____

_____

_____

2.  La ciudad

_____

_____

_____

_____

3. Una ocurrencia heroica

_____

_____

_____

**Realidades 2**

**Capítulo 5A**

Nombre

Hora

Fecha

**WRITING**

## Actividad 11

You are working as a reporter for the school newspaper and are trying to get the facts about several different stories. Read the headlines below and write the questions you need to ask in order to round out your reports. Follow the model.

**Modelo** **EL EQUIPO DE BÁSQUETBOL GANÓ AYER**

*¿Qué hora era cuando empezó el partido?*

*¿Quién y cómo era el otro equipo?*

*¿Cómo se sentía el equipo de nuestra escuela cuando ganó?*

1. **NUESTRA ESCUELA #2 EN EL CONCURSO DE MATEMÁTICAS**

2. **EL PRINCIPAL DECLARÓ: ¡NO SE PERMITE LLEVAR PANTALONES CORTOS!**

3. **¡EL BAILE DE LA ESCUELA UN ÉXITO!**

4. **JONES Y RULFO GANARON LAS ELECCIONES**

5. **¡INCENDIO EN LA CAFETERÍA!**

**Realidades** 2

**Capítulo 5A**

Nombre _____

Hora _____

Fecha _____

**WRITING**

## Actividad 12

Your local television station's news reporters are investigating two stories from last night and want to talk to people who witnessed the events. Using the pictures provided, write what a witness would say to a reporter about each scene. Follow the model.

**Modelo**   La señora Alfonso _oyó los perros ladrando (barking)_ .

1. Enrique y Roberto _____.

2. El incendio _____.

3. Tú _____.

4. Ignacio _____.

5. El ladrón (robber) _____.

6. Marisol y yo _____.

7. Yo _____.

## Actividad 13

**A.** You want to write a mystery story about a crime that took place in a small town. In order to start developing the plot, answer the questions below using your imagination.

1. ¿Qué hora era y dónde estabas? _____

2. ¿Qué era el ruido (*noise*) que oíste? _____

3. ¿Cómo era el hombre que viste? ¿Qué hizo? _____

4. ¿Qué tenía en su mochila? _____

5. ¿Qué hora era cuando empezó el incendio? _____

6. ¿A qué hora llegaron los bomberos? _____

7. ¿Qué hiciste después? _____

**B.** Now, organize your answers into a short description of the plot of your story. You may wish to add details or connecting words to make it flow well. Be creative!

_____

_____

_____

_____

_____

_____

_____

_____

_____

_____

_____

_____

_____

**Realidades 2**

**Capítulo 5B**

Nombre _____

Hora _____

Fecha _____

**VIDEO**

# Antes de ver el video

## Actividad 1

When do you need to stay in bed because you are sick, and when do you need to go to the hospital? Write three examples for each. The first ones have been done for you.

| ¿Cuándo me quedo en cama? | ¿Cuándo voy al hospital? |
|---|---|
| Cuando tengo un dolor de cabeza muy fuerte | Cuando me lastimo el brazo |
| | |
| | |
| | |

# ¿Comprendes?

## Actividad 2

Identify the speaker of each of the following quotes from the video.

1. "Si no hay un terremoto él no se despierta ..."  _____

2. "¡Qué lástima! ... ¿Y Tomás?"  _____

3. "¡Ay, Dios mío!"  _____

4. "¿Qué pasó entonces?"  _____

5. "¡Pobre Tomás!"  _____

6. "¡El pobrecito soy yo!"  _____

7. "¡No debes despertarte a las tres de la mañana!"  _____

8. "¿Por qué no me dijeron nada?"  _____

## Actividad 3

Look at each video scene and write one or two complete sentences to tell what is happening.

1. _____

_____

**Realidades 2**

**Capítulo 5B**

Nombre

Hora

Fecha

**VIDEO**

**2.** _____

**3.** _____

**4.** _____

**5.** _____

**6.** _____

## Y, ¿qué más?

### Actividad 4

Have you ever had a silly accident? What happened? Answer the questions about your accident or the accident of someone you know.

**1.** ¿Qué hacías cuando ocurrió el accidente?

_____

_____

**2.** ¿Te lastimaste algo?

_____

_____

**3.** ¿Fuiste a la sala de emergencia? ¿Qué pasó?

_____

_____

**Realidades** ②

**Capítulo 5B**

Nombre _____

Hora _____

Fecha _____

**AUDIO**

## Actividad 5

Your friend Juan Luis just spent his first day as a volunteer in the local hospital's emergency room. Listen as he tells his parents what happened. Write the number of the description in the corresponding circle in the picture below. You will hear each description twice.

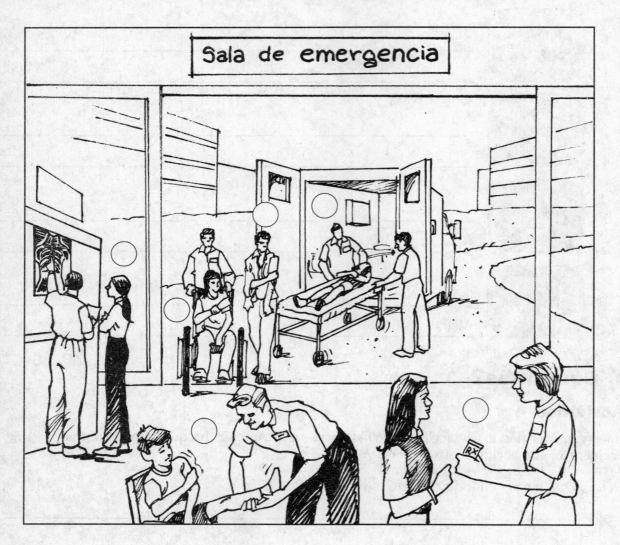

**Realidades 2**

**Capítulo 5B**

Nombre _____

Hora _____

Fecha _____

**AUDIO**

## Actividad 6

Listen as several teenagers talk about what happened when they were injured recently. Match what each describes to one of the pictures below. Write the corresponding letter in the blanks below. You will hear each description twice.

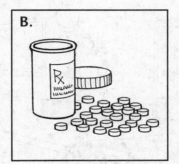

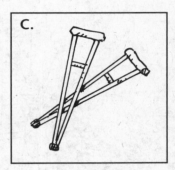

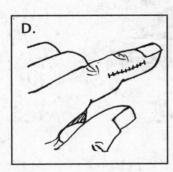

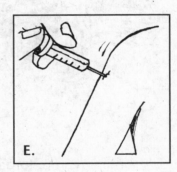

1. _____   2. _____   3. _____   4. _____   5. _____

## Actividad 7

A popular **telenovela** added a new character to the cast of people who work at the fictitious hospital in the show. The character, Lola Loca, was added to give humor to the show. Many of the things she does are illogical and silly. Just listen to the things she did last week on the show! Fill in the grid below to show how you would categorize her actions. You will hear each statement twice.

|          | 1 | 2 | 3 | 4 | 5 | 6 | 7 | 8 |
|----------|---|---|---|---|---|---|---|---|
| **Lógico**  |   |   |   |   |   |   |   |   |
| **Ilógico** |   |   |   |   |   |   |   |   |

**Realidades 2**

**Capítulo 5B**

Nombre

Fecha

Hora

**AUDIO**

## Actividad 8

A group of friends was recalling what each was doing when the police arrived at the scene of an accident. Write the number of the statement in the corresponding circle in the picture below. You will hear each statement twice.

## Actividad 9

As a counselor at a boy's summer camp, Jorge is the person to whom the children report any accidents or injuries. Listen as children run to Jorge and tell him what campers were doing when a recent injury occurred. Take notes in the grid below about what happened to each child. You will hear each set of statements twice.

| Nombre del niño | ¿Qué estaba haciendo el niño? | ¿Qué se lastimó? |
|---|---|---|
| Jaime | | |
| Luis | | |
| Cristóbal | | |
| Óscar | | |
| Félix | | |

Nombre _____     Hora _____

Fecha _____

WRITING

## Actividad 10

The school nurse is explaining to some students situations in which they might need the medical treatments pictured below. Write what you might say about each treatment. Follow the model.

Modelo

_Necesitas un yeso cuando te caes de la escalera y te rompes la pierna._

1. _____

2. _____

3. _____

4. _____

5. _____

6. _____

7. _____

**Realidades 2**

**Capítulo 5B**

Nombre _____

Hora _____

Fecha _____

**WRITING**

## Actividad 11

Carmela is writing in her diary after a busy day. Look at the pictures below of what she and her friends did, and write short diary entries based on each one. Follow the model.

**Modelo**   Javier _le dijo la verdad a su padre. No pudo mentirle a_ _su papá._

1. Mariel _____
   _____

2. Elena y yo _____
   _____

3. Mis hermanos _____
   _____

4. Ayer yo _____
   _____

5. El cartero _____
   _____

6. A las nueve los estudiantes _____
   _____

**Realidades** ② 

**Capítulo 5B**

Nombre _____

Fecha _____

Hora _____

**WRITING**

## Actividad 12

On Friday the 13th, lots of people had bad luck. Tell what the people below were doing when something bad happened. Use the imperfect progressive tense and be creative. Follow the model.

Modelo    Yo me torcí el tobillo.

*Yo estaba corriendo en el parque y no vi el plátano en la calle.  Me caí.*

1. Marcos se rompió la pierna. _____

_____

2. Luisa y su mamá chocaron con una bicicleta. _____

_____

3. ¡Yo salí de la casa sin pantalones y sin mis llaves! _____

_____

4. Tú te lastimaste la cabeza. _____

_____

5. El camarero rompió todos los platos. _____

_____

6. Nosotros tropezamos con los juguetes en el piso de la sala. _____

_____

7. Paco y Ramón se cortaron los dedos. _____

_____

8. Marta y yo nos enfermamos. _____

_____

9. Yo choqué con otro estudiante en la escuela. _____

_____

10. Tú te torciste la muñeca izquierda. _____

_____

**Realidades 2**

**Capítulo 5B**

Nombre _____

Hora _____

Fecha _____

**WRITING**

## Actividad 13

Julieta is a girl who likes to do too many things at once. Last week, her hectic lifestyle finally caught up with her.

**A.** Look at the picture below and describe at least four activities Julieta was doing at the same time. Follow the model.

| Modelo | _Julieta estaba leyendo._ |

1. _____
2. _____
3. _____
4. _____
5. _____

**B.** Now, think about a hectic day you or someone you know had recently. Write five sentences to tell what happened. Follow the model.

| Modelo | _Mi hermana Julia estaba caminando y comiendo cuando se cayó y se lastimó la cabeza._ |

1. _____
   _____
2. _____
   _____
3. _____
   _____
4. _____
   _____
5. _____
   _____

**Realidades 2**

**Capítulo 6A**

Nombre _____

Hora _____

Fecha _____

**VIDEO**

# Antes de ver el video

## Actividad 1

In this video you will hear an interview with a famous soccer player. Write six sentences the player might use to describe what happened in a recent game. Follow the model.

Modelo   *El jugador metió un gol.* _____

1. _____     4. _____

2. _____     5. _____

3. _____     6. _____

# ¿Comprendes?

## Actividad 2

Read the following statements about the video and decide whether they are **cierto** or **falso**. If the statement is true, write **cierto**.  If **falso,** rewrite the statement to make it true.

1. Manolo y Ramón están viendo una entrevista en la tele.

   _____

2. Claudia tiene interés en la entrevista de Luis Campos.

   _____

3. Luis Campos es el mejor jugador de las Águilas del América.

   _____

4. Manolo y Ramón tienen planes para ir al partido de hoy.

   _____

5. Claudia sabe cómo pueden ver el partido en el estadio.

   _____

6. Manolo y Ramón no quieren ir con Claudia al estadio para ver el partido.

   _____

**VIDEO**

## Actividad 3

Do you remember what happened in the video? Using the pictures to help you, summarize the video in your own words. Follow the model.

| Modelo | _Manolo y Ramón vieron una entrevista con "la Pantera", Luis Campos._ |

1. _____
_____

2. _____
_____

3. _____
_____

4. _____
_____

## Y, ¿qué más?

## Actividad 4

If you were a reporter for the school newspaper, who would you interview? Why? Answer these questions. Then, write five questions you would ask during the interview. Follow the model.

| Modelo | _Voy a entrevistar a la presidenta del club de español. Quiero saber las actividades que planea para el semestre._ |

_____

_____

_____

_____

_____

**Realidades 2**

**Capítulo 6A**

Nombre

Hora

Fecha

**AUDIO**

## Actividad 5

The popular radio program **"Nuestra comunidad"** is highlighting three successful young women from the local Spanish-speaking community. As you listen to parts of their interviews, use the pictures below to decide whether the young woman speaking is Laura, Flor, or Isabel. Then, write the name of the young woman in the corresponding space. You will hear each set of statements twice.

| Laura | Flor | Isabel |
|---|---|---|

 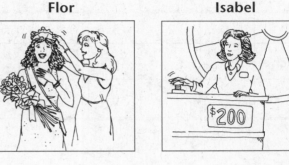

1. _____   3. _____   5. _____   7. _____

2. _____   4. _____   6. _____   8. _____

## Actividad 6

In the past few years there has been a growing interest in women's soccer. Listen as Don Balón interviews Eva Barca, a rising women's soccer star. As you hear the different segments of the interview, read the following statements and tell whether each is **cierto** or **falso.** You will hear each segment twice.

| | | |
|---|---|---|
| **1.** Eva Barca escucha el programa de Don Balón. | **Cierto** | **Falso** |
| **2.** Don Balón sólo entrevista a las mujeres. | **Cierto** | **Falso** |
| **3.** Las mujeres ganan más dinero que los hombres. | **Cierto** | **Falso** |
| **4.** Hay un muñeco de Eva Barca. | **Cierto** | **Falso** |
| **5.** Según Eva, no hay muñecos de los hombres jugadores. | **Cierto** | **Falso** |
| **6.** Según Eva, su entrenador grita demasiado. | **Cierto** | **Falso** |
| **7.** Según Eva, los aficionados son iguales para las dos ligas. | **Cierto** | **Falso** |

Nombre _____  Hora _____

Fecha _____

## Actividad 7

How do contestants spend their free time during the "**Señorita América del Sur**" beauty pageant? Listen as some women talk about what their friend(s) in the pageant did last night, and as others talk about what they are doing today to calm themselves before the final competition begins. As you listen to each contestant, decide whether she is talking about last night or today. You will hear each set of statements twice.

|        | 1 | 2 | 3 | 4 | 5 | 6 | 7 | 8 |
|--------|---|---|---|---|---|---|---|---|
| **Anoche** |   |   |   |   |   |   |   |   |
| **Hoy**    |   |   |   |   |   |   |   |   |

## Actividad 8

Even though pets cannot express their emotions through words, they can express themselves through their actions. As you hear each person describe his or her pet's behavior, match a picture to the pet. Write the number of each pet owner's description underneath the picture of his or her dog. You will hear each description twice.

_____

_____

_____

_____

_____

_____

**Realidades** ②

**Capítulo 6A**

Nombre _____

Hora _____

Fecha _____

**AUDIO**

## Actividad 9

Yesterday in her popular talk show **"Dime la verdad,"** Lola Lozano had as her guests a group of famous soccer players. The question on the program was **"¿Qué lo vuelve más loco?"** In the table below, take notes about what each one said. Then, use your notes to complete the sentences about each guest. You will hear each conversation twice.

**MIS NOTAS**

1.

2.

3.

4.

5.

1. Luis se vuelve loco cuando _____.

2. Marisol se vuelve loca cuando _____.

3. Enrique se vuelve loco cuando _____.

4. María se vuelve loca cuando _____

_____.

5. Martín se vuelve loco cuando _____.

**Realidades 2**

**Capítulo 6A**

Nombre _____

Hora _____

Fecha _____

**WRITING**

## Actividad 10

You and your friend are flipping through the channels, and you have each found one thing that you'd like to watch. Using the pictures below, describe each show in detail. The first description has been started for you.

1.

  *Es el campeonato de la Liga Internacional de Tenis.*
  _____
  _____
  _____
  _____

2.

  _____
  _____
  _____
  _____

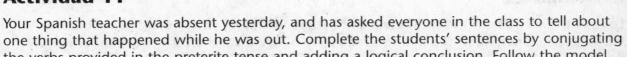

**Realidades 2**

**Capítulo 6A**

Nombre _____

Hora _____

Fecha _____

**WRITING**

## Actividad 11

Your Spanish teacher was absent yesterday, and has asked everyone in the class to tell about one thing that happened while he was out. Complete the students' sentences by conjugating the verbs provided in the preterite tense and adding a logical conclusion. Follow the model.

**Modelo**   nosotros / competir

_Nosotros competimos en un concurso de belleza para practicar las_
_palabras para describir la ropa._

1. yo / servir

   _____

2. Elena / sentirse

   _____

3. todos nosotros / repetir

   _____

4. Jacques / dormir

   _____

5. tú / reírse

   _____

6. Lola y Raquel / pedir

   _____

7. Pancho y él / sonreír

   _____

8. Susana / mentir

   _____

9. yo / seguir

   _____

10. nosotros / divertirse

    _____

**WRITING**

## Actividad 12

Look at the scene below from Mariela and Pablo's wedding. Write at least six sentences to tell what is happening at the moment. You may want to use the verbs **casarse**, **enojarse**, **ponerse**, **aburrirse**, **dormirse**, and **divertirse**.

_____

_____

_____

_____

_____

_____

_____

_____

_____

_____

_____

Nombre _____  Hora _____

Fecha _____

## Actividad 13

Juanita just participated in a beauty pageant, and is writing a letter to her grandmother to tell her what it was like.

**A.** First, write sentences to help her describe where the event took place, who was there, and what everyone looked like. The first one is done for you.

*Estuve en el Teatro Central.* _____  _____

_____  _____

_____  _____

_____  _____

**B.** Next, list what Juanita and the other contestants probably did during the competition. The first one is done for you.

*Yo me vestí en una hora.* _____  _____

_____  _____

_____  _____

**C.** Finally, use your sentences from Part A and Part B to help Juanita write her letter to her grandmother. The letter has been started for you.

*Querida abuela:*

*Hoy yo participé en un concurso de belleza. ¡Fue fantástico!*

_____

_____

_____

_____

_____

_____

_____

_____

**Realidades 2**

**Capítulo 6B**

Nombre _____

Hora _____

Fecha _____

**VIDEO**

# Antes de ver el video

## Actividad 1

The next video is about a short movie that Manolo directs. Think about movies you have seen recently and answer the following questions using words from your vocabulary.

1. ¿Qué clase de película fue? _____

2. ¿Quiénes eran los actores principales? _____

   _____

3. ¿Quién era el (la) director(a)? _____

4. ¿De qué trataba? _____

   _____

5. ¿Había mucha violencia o era más un cuento de enamorados?

   _____

# ¿Comprendes?

## Actividad 2

Answer the following questions in complete sentences in order to better understand the video.

1. ¿Qué está haciendo Ramón en su habitación?

   _____

   _____

2. ¿Quién entra a la habitación cuando Ramón está estudiando?

   _____

   _____

**Realidades** 2

**Capítulo 6B**

Nombre _____

Hora _____

Fecha _____

VIDEO

**3.** ¿Qué quiere hacer Ramón con el periódico?

_____

_____

**4.** ¿En qué idiomas puede hablar el mosquito?

_____

_____

**5.** ¿Por qué Ramón no mata el mosquito?

_____

_____

**6.** ¿Dónde se va a esconder el mosquito el día del examen para explicarle todo a Ramón?

_____

_____

**7.** ¿Quién mata el mosquito y cómo lo hace?

_____

_____

## Actividad 3

In the chart below are quotes from the video. Next to each quote, write the name of the character who said it and the role he or she played in the movie. Follow the model.

| Frase u oración | Personaje | Papel |
|---|---|---|
| Modelo "¡¡¡NOOOOOOOO!!!" | Claudia | mosquito |
| 1. "Tengo que estudiar y tú me molestas." | | |
| 2. "¡Yo quiero hacer el personaje principal!" | | |
| 3. "¡Ramón, despiértate ya!" | | |
| 4. "A ver... necesito tres actores." | | |
| 5. "¡No, no me mates, por favor!" | | |
| 6. "¿Podemos tener efectos especiales?" | | |
| 7. "Parece que estudiaste mucho." | | |
| 8. "Pero, Teresa, ¿qué has hecho?" | | |

# Y, ¿qué más?

## Actividad 4

Now that you have seen the movie made by the characters from the video, think about a film that you might like to create. In the spaces below, list the characters and describe the plot and the scene to get you started.

Los personajes: _____

_____

_____

El argumento: _____

_____

_____

_____

La escena: _____

_____

_____

_____

Nombre _____     Hora _____

Fecha _____     **AUDIO**

## Actividad 5

The drama class is trying to decide on the cast of their upcoming spring production "**Aquella noche.**" Match the name of the person with his or her suggested role by marking an X in the corresponding square in the grid. You will hear each set of statements twice.

|  | El (la) ladrón (ladrona) | El galán | El (la) extra-terrestre | El (la) detective | El (la) director(a) | La víctima |
|---|---|---|---|---|---|---|
| Fernando |  |  |  |  |  |  |
| María |  |  |  |  |  |  |
| Matilde |  |  |  |  |  |  |
| Antonio |  |  |  |  |  |  |
| Alberto |  |  |  |  |  |  |
| Carmen |  |  |  |  |  |  |

## Actividad 6

Listen as people talk about movies they have seen. As you hear each opinion, fill in the grid below by writing or circling the correct answer. You do not need to write complete sentences. You will hear each set of statements twice.

|  | ¿La recomienda? | ¿El argumento? | ¿Qué cosa(s) le gustó/gustaron más? |
|---|---|---|---|
| 1. | Sí / No | Básico / Complicado |  |
| 2. | Sí / No | Básico / Complicado |  |
| 3. | Sí / No | Básico / Complicado |  |
| 4. | Sí / No | Básico / Complicado |  |
| 5. | Sí / No | Básico / Complicado |  |

**Realidades 2**

**Capítulo 6B**

Nombre _____

Fecha _____

Hora _____

**AUDIO**

## Actividad 7

In today's episode of **"Dime la verdad,"** Lola Lana interviews actors and actresses on the set of a popular **telenovela**. She quickly learns that they all have very different movie preferences. As you listen, write the number of the interview underneath the corresponding poster. You will hear each set of statements twice.

_____    _____    _____

_____    _____

## Actividad 8

Even though Julia's grandmother only missed one episode of her favorite **telenovela**, she is eager to hear about what she missed. As Julia tells her about the last episode, answer the questions below about what has happened with each character. You will hear each conversation twice.

¿Qué ha pasado?

**1.** Javier _____

**2.** Marlena _____

**3.** Marco _____

**4.** Victoria _____

**5.** Marisol _____

**Realidades 2**

**Capítulo 6B**

Nombre _____

Fecha _____

Hora _____

**AUDIO**

## Actividad 9

You and your classmates are creating storyboards to outline the plots of your upcoming class movies. Listen as one student describes the plot line for his project. Take notes on each part of the plot in the top half of each of the storyboard boxes below. Then, draw a quick sketch in the bottom half of each box. You will hear the story twice.

| NOTES and SKETCHES | | | |
|---|---|---|---|
| #1 | #2 | #3 | #4 |
| #5 | #6 | #7 | #8 |

**Realidades 2**

**Capítulo 6B**

Nombre _____

Hora _____

Fecha _____

**WRITING**

## Actividad 10

Look at the movie theater marquee below. For each movie, write at least three sentences to tell what you think it might be about. The first one has been started for you.

1. "Un verano que recordar" es una película romántica. _____

_____

_____

2. _____

_____

_____

_____

3. _____

_____

_____

_____

**Realidades 2**

**Capítulo 6B**

Nombre _____

Hora _____

Fecha _____

**WRITING**

## Actividad 11

**A.** You are interested in hosting an exchange student from Spain. Fill out the form below so that your school can find you a compatible student.

Nombre _____

Edad *(age)* _____

Actividad(es) que te gusta(n) _____

Comida(s) que te encanta(n) _____

Clase(s) que te interesa(n) _____

Tipo(s) de película(s) que te fascina(n) _____

Cosa(s) que te disgusta(n) _____

**B.** Now, read Ramiro's form below and write complete sentences to compare your interests with his. Follow the model.

Nombre *Ramiro Fuentes*

Edad *16*

Actividad(es) que te gusta(n) *esquiar, leer, ir al cine*

Comida(s) que te encanta(n) *la carne, la pasta, los pasteles*

Clase(s) que te interesa(n) *ciencias naturales, inglés*

Tipo(s) de película(s) que te fascina(n) *románticas, de horror*

Cosa(s) que te disgusta(n) *la televisión, los gatos*

**Modelo** *A Ramiro le gusta leer pero a mí me disgusta. Prefiero más escribir.*

1. _____

2. _____

3. _____

4. _____

5. _____

**C.** Based on your interests, do you think you and Ramiro are compatible? Why or why not? Write your answer in Spanish in one or two complete sentences.

_____

_____

**Realidades 2**

**Capítulo 6B**

Nombre _____

Hora _____

Fecha _____

**WRITING**

## Actividad 12

Before becoming a host family to a Mexican exchange student, your family is asked to provide a list of things you have done to become familiar with Mexican culture. Under each category below, write three sentences about your real or imaginary experiences. The first one has been done for you.

**Los viajes**

Nosotros *hemos viajado a Cancún y hemos visitado las ruinas mayas.* _____

Yo _____

Mi hermano _____

**Los deportes**

Mi familia y yo _____

Mi clase de español _____

Mis padres _____

**Las clases**

Yo _____

Mi hermano(a) _____

Mis hermanos(as) _____

**Las comidas**

Mi madre _____

Yo _____

Toda la familia _____

**Realidades 2**

**Capítulo 6B**

Nombre

Hora

Fecha

**WRITING**

## Actividad 13

You are writing a review for the school newspaper of a movie that you saw recently.

**A.** First, write down the information requested below to give some background information about the movie. You may use your imagination.

1. Nombre del actor principal _____

   Otras películas de él _____

2. Nombre de la actriz principal _____

   Otras películas de ella _____

3. Nombre del director (de la directora) _____

   Otras películas de él (ella) _____

**B.** Now, write five sentences about your opinion of the movie. Tell what you liked, what you disliked, what interested you, etc. about the plot, acting, and directing of the movie.

_____

_____

_____

_____

_____

**C.** Now, write your review for the paper, using the information from Part A and Part B to help you.

_____

_____

_____

_____

_____

_____

_____

**Realidades 2**

**Capítulo 7A**

Nombre _____

Fecha _____

Hora _____

**VIDEO**

# Antes de ver el video

## Actividad 1

List eight ingredients that you would need to prepare your favorite dish.

_____   _____

_____   _____

_____   _____

# ¿Comprendes?

## Actividad 2

Javier is teaching Ignacio how to make paella. The steps he takes and the things he tells Ignacio are listed below, but they are in the wrong order. Order them correctly by writing a **1** to indicate the first thing Javier said and a **7** to indicate the last thing he said.

**a.** _____ ¡No tires el aceite! Y no añadas más. Ya tienes más que suficiente.

**b.** _____ No uso ingredientes congelados. Sólo uso ingredientes frescos... por eso mi paella es tan rica.

**c.** _____ Bueno, está bien. Pero primero vamos al supermercado..., a comprar los ingredientes.

**d.** _____ Primero tienes que calentar el aceite, en una sartén grande; como ésta.

**e.** _____ No te olvides del aceite, y no dejes que se caliente demasiado.

**f.** _____ Quieres decir, vamos a volver a empezar otra vez...

**g.** _____ Quiero preparar una comida especial para Ana, para su cumpleaños.

**Realidades 2**

**Capítulo 7A**

Nombre _____

Hora _____

Fecha _____

**VIDEO**

## Actividad 3

You have just finished watching Javier and Ignacio have a cooking adventure. Answer the questions below in complete sentences. Follow the model.

Modelo   ¿Adónde van Javier e Ignacio?

*Ignacio y Javier van al supermercado a comprar los ingredientes para hacer una paella.*

1.   ¿Qué sabe cocinar Ignacio?

_____

2.   ¿Cómo es la paella de Javier? ¿Por qué?

_____

_____

3.   ¿Qué van a necesitar los jóvenes para hacer la paella?

_____

4.   ¿Dónde se prepara la paella?

_____

_____

5.   ¿Qué tiene que hacer Ignacio con los ajos antes de cocinarlos?

_____

_____

Nombre _____

Hora _____

Fecha _____

6. ¿Por qué piensa Javier que Ana va a recibir una gran sorpresa, que no va a ser buena?

_____

_____

# Y, ¿qué más?

## Actividad 4

Do you like to have big dinner parties or intimate dinners for two? What would you prepare for such a dinner? Write a short paragraph to tell about your ideal gathering and its menu. Follow the model.

| Modelo | *A mí me gusta reunirme con mis mejores amigos.* |
|---|---|

*En estas reuniones, me gusta cocinar algo como un pescado en salsa de queso. Invito a varios amigos, y ellos traen los otros platos: la ensalada, la bebida y el postre.*

*Nos ponemos a cocinar todos, y escuchamos música mientras preparamos la cena. Al terminar, todos comemos una comida muy rica, y todos quedamos contentos de compartir una noche tan agradable.*

_____

_____

_____

_____

_____

_____

**Realidades** ② 
**Capítulo 7A**

Nombre _____

Fecha _____

Hora _____

**AUDIO**

## Actividad 5

Alejandro's older sister has been trying to teach him the basics of cooking. Listen to the questions he asks her during one of their phone conversations. If the question seems logical, circle the word **lógico** and if the question seems illogical, circle the word **ilógico.** You will hear each question twice.

1. lógico    ilógico          5. lógico    ilógico

2. lógico    ilógico          6. lógico    ilógico

3. lógico    ilógico          7. lógico    ilógico

4. lógico    ilógico          8. lógico    ilógico

## Actividad 6

Both Ignacio and Javier think they are expert cooks. As they are preparing paella, each wants to make sure the other is doing it right. Listen to their conversations, and match each one to one of the pictures below. Write the number of the conversation in the blank underneath the corresponding picture. You will hear each conversation twice.

**Realidades 2**

**Capítulo 7A**

Nombre _____

Hora _____

Fecha _____

**AUDIO**

## Actividad 7

Listen as different people give Roberto advice about cooking. As you listen to each piece of advice, decide whether the person is advising him on: a) getting ready to cook; b) things to do while he's cooking; or c) things to do after he's finished cooking. Place an **X** in the appropriate box in the grid below. You will hear each piece of advice twice.

|  | 1 | 2 | 3 | 4 | 5 | 6 | 7 | 8 | 9 | 10 |
|---|---|---|---|---|---|---|---|---|---|---|
| Antes de cocinar... |  |  |  |  |  |  |  |  |  |  |
| Cuando cocinas... |  |  |  |  |  |  |  |  |  |  |
| Después de cocinar... |  |  |  |  |  |  |  |  |  |  |

## Actividad 8

Listen as a counselor at a Spanish Immersion Camp tells the campers what things are going to be like at the camp for the summer. Draw a circle around the things that do happen, and an **X** over the pictures of the things that don't happen. You will hear each statement twice.

**Realidades 2**

**Capítulo 7A**

Nombre _____

Hora _____

Fecha _____

**AUDIO**

## Actividad 9

Ryan's friend, Carmen, asks him to come to dinner at her home. Some of the things he eats are very familiar, but others are not. Listen as they talk about what is on the dinner table. Write the number of each conversation under the corresponding item on the dinner table. You will hear each conversation twice.

Nombre _____

Hora _____

Fecha _____

## Actividad 10

Your mother is running late and calls you from the store to tell you to get dinner started. Use the pictures below to write what she tells you to do. Follow the model.

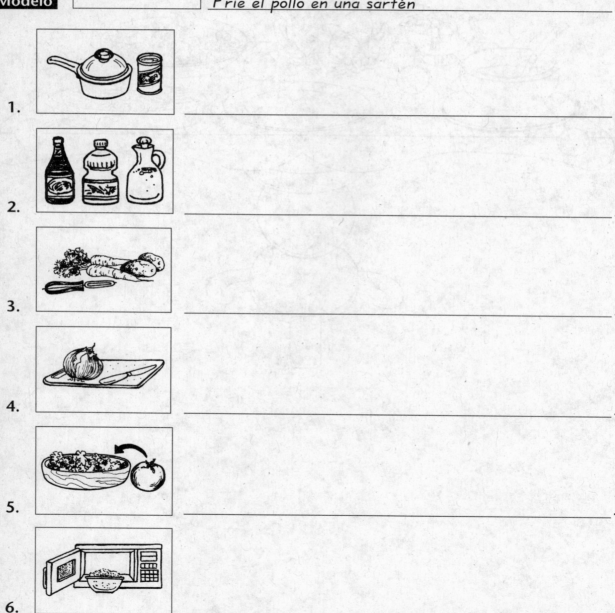

 **Modelo**    *Fríe el pollo en una sartén* .

1. _____ .

2. _____ .

3. _____ .

4. _____ .

5. _____ .

6. _____ .

Nombre _____ Hora _____

Fecha _____

## Actividad 11

Pancho is sick and goes to the doctor, who tells him what *not* to do if he wants to get better quickly. Write the doctor's instructions using the verbs below and your imagination. Follow the model.

| hablar | comer | beber | ir |
|--------|-------|-------|-----|
| ser | dormir | empezar | jugar |

**Modelo**   *No comas ni las papas fritas ni los pasteles cuando estás enfermo.*

1. _____

2. _____

3. _____

4. _____

5. _____

6. _____

7. _____

8. _____

**WRITING**

## Actividad 12

A Spanish-speaking friend wants you to mail her your recipe for gazpacho. You are looking at the recipe card in your files, but decide it would be better to write out the instructions in addition to the information on the file. Write out instructions for how to prepare the gazpacho, as shown in the first item.

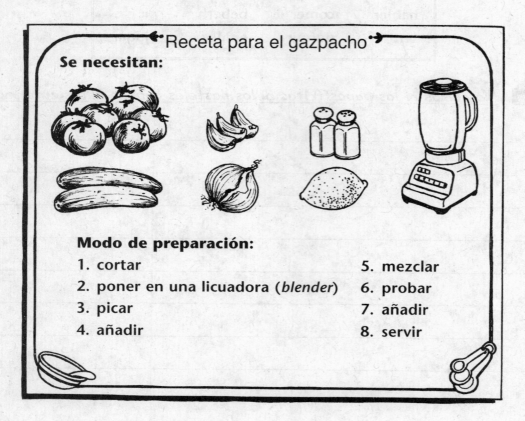

**Receta para el gazpacho**

**Se necesitan:**

**Modo de preparación:**

1. cortar
2. poner en una licuadora (*blender*)
3. picar
4. añadir

5. mezclar
6. probar
7. añadir
8. servir

1. _Se cortan el pepino (cucumber) y los tomates_____.

2. _____.

3. _____.

4. _____.

5. _____.

6. _____.

7. _____.

8. _____.

Nombre _____ Hora _____

Fecha _____ **WRITING**

## Actividad 13

**A.** Your school is opening up a kitchen for students to use. Help the administration set rules for its use by first writing a list of the things that one can and should do there. Follow the model.

Modelo  *Se usa el microondas para recalentar la comida* _____ .

1. _____ .

2. _____ .

3. _____ .

4. _____ .

5. _____ .

6. _____ .

**B.** Now, set limits by writing a list of six things that students should *not* do there. Follow the model.

Modelo  *No tires la comida en la cocina* _____ .

1. _____ .

2. _____ .

3. _____ .

4. _____ .

5. _____ .

6. _____ .

Nombre _____     Hora _____

Fecha _____     **VIDEO**

# Antes de ver el video

## Actividad 1

Make a list of six things you would bring to a picnic.

1. _____     4. _____
2. _____     5. _____
3. _____     6. _____

Now, name three activities you might do on a picnic.

1. _____
2. _____
3. _____

Finally, name two things that could happen to spoil your picnic.

1. _____

   _____

2. _____

   _____

# ¿Comprendes?

## Actividad 2

All of the following sentences are incorrect. Rewrite them to make them correct.

1. Manolo es del campo y no le gusta comer en la ciudad.

   _____

2. Claudia trae en la canasta toda la comida que preparó.

   _____

**Realidades 2**

**Capítulo 7B**

Nombre _____

Hora _____

Fecha _____

**VIDEO**

**3.** Los muchachos van al parque en el coche de Claudia.

_____

**4.** En el parque nadie hace fogatas.

_____

**5.** En el parque no hay puestos de comida; no pueden comprar nada.

_____

**6.** A Manolo le encanta la comida que hace Claudia.

_____

## Actividad 3

Answer the following questions in complete sentences based on the video.

**1.** ¿Por qué a Manolo no le gusta comer en el campo?

_____

**2.** ¿Por qué Claudia no puede darles bebidas a los amigos?

_____

**3.** ¿Por qué escogen un sitio para sentarse por fin?

_____

**4.** ¿Quiénes dan una caminata por el parque?

_____

**5.** ¿Qué comida trajo Claudia? ¿Por qué?

_____

Nombre _____

Hora _____

Fecha _____

**VIDEO**

# Y, ¿qué más?

## Actividad 4

Picnics are a fun summer activity. Make a list telling what kind of food and beverage you like to bring to a picnic, who you like to invite, and where you like to have it. Use complete sentences. The first one has been done for you.

1. _Me gusta traer una canasta con mucha comida cuando quiero hacer un picnic._

2. _____

3. _____

4. _____

5. _____

6. _____

7. _____

Nombre _____ Hora _____

Fecha _____

## Actividad 5

The Cruz and Ramos families are getting together for their annual barbecue. Listen as they talk about what they brought in their picnic baskets. As you listen to each family member talk about a particular food item, look at the pictures below of the picnic baskets. Then, write **C** in the blank if you think a member of the Cruz family is speaking, and write **R** in the blank if you think a member of the Ramos family is speaking. You will hear each set of statements twice.

1. _____    5. _____

2. _____    6. _____

3. _____    7. _____

4. _____    8. _____

**Realidades 2**

**Capítulo 7B**

Nombre _____

Hora _____

Fecha _____

**AUDIO**

## Actividad 6

Some people prefer the great outdoors and others prefer the comforts of being indoors. As you listen to each conversation, determine whether the person is talking about eating outdoors or inside at a restaurant. Fill in the grid below as you listen. You will hear each set of statements twice.

| | 1 | 2 | 3 | 4 | 5 | 6 |
|---|---|---|---|---|---|---|
| | | | | | | |
| | | | | | | |

## Actividad 7

You are helping the Scoutmaster, Sr. Naranjo, assign tasks for the boys in his troop to do at summer camp. Your job is to write each task in the chart below so that each pair of boys knows what to do. You will hear each task twice.

| Carlos y Ramón | Lleven los sacos de dormir. |
|---|---|
| 1. Dani y Benito | |
| 2. Adán y Miguel | |
| 3. David y Enrique | |
| 4. Jaime y Pepe | |
| 5. Arturo y Benito | |
| 6. Raúl y Tomás | |

Nombre _____ Hora _____

Fecha _____ **AUDIO**

## Actividad 8

Listen as people talk about what they did on behalf of their friends or relatives last week. As you listen to each conversation, fill in the grid below with the following information: 1) what he or she did; 2) on whose behalf he or she did it; and 3) the amount of time it took. For the first column, choose from the following statements: **a) Preparó una cena; b) Trabajó en una computadora; c) Estudió matemáticas; d) Limpió el apartamento.** You will hear each set of statements twice.

| | ¿Qué hizo? | ¿Por quién lo hizo? | ¿Por cuánto tiempo lo hizo? |
|---|---|---|---|
| 1. | | | _____ horas |
| 2. | | | _____ horas |
| 3. | | | _____ horas |
| 4. | | | _____ horas |

## Actividad 9

Listen as guests on a cruise ship listen to instructions from the Activity Director about the upcoming "ship-to-shore" camping trip. She gives lots of advice on what to do on their expedition. As you listen to each piece of advice, decide whether she is talking about trekking in the woods or getting ready for the evening barbecue and bonfire. Put an X in the correct box below. You will hear each piece of advice twice.

| | 1 | 2 | 3 | 4 | 5 | 6 | 7 | 8 | 9 | 10 |
|---|---|---|---|---|---|---|---|---|---|---|
| Consejos para el caminante | | | | | | | | | | |
| Consejos para hacer una barbacoa y fogata | | | | | | | | | | |

**Realidades 2**

**Capítulo 7B**

Nombre _____

Fecha _____

Hora _____

**WRITING**

## Actividad 10

Look at the picture below of the picnic Adriana recently had with her family. Help her write a letter to her pen pal describing the picnic. The letter has been started for you.

Querida Laura,

    <u>Mi familia y yo decidimos comer al aire libre porque hacía sol ese día.</u>

_____

_____

_____

_____

_____

_____

_____

Saludos,

*Adriana*

Nombre _____

Hora _____

Fecha _____

**WRITING**

## Actividad 11

Your teachers are making lists of rules for their classrooms.  For each class below, write four rules. Write two rules about what the students have to do in the class, and two about what the teacher must do in the class. Follow the model.

1. **TECNOLOGÍA**
   los estudiantes
   *No traigan ni comida ni bebidas a la clase.* _____

   _____

   el (la) profesor(a)
   *Empiece la clase a tiempo.* _____

   _____

2. **ARTE**
   los estudiantes
   _____

   _____

   el (la) profesor(a)
   _____

   _____

3. **EDUCACIÓN FÍSICA**
   los estudiantes
   _____

   _____

   el (la) profesor(a)
   _____

   _____

4. **BIOLOGÍA**
   los estudiantes
   _____

   _____

   el (la) profesor(a)
   _____

   _____

## Actividad 12

Answer the following questions in complete sentences that include the word **por**, where applicable.

1. ¿Qué fue la última cosa que compraste? ¿Cuánto pagaste?

   _____

2. Por lo general, ¿gastas mucho cuando vas de compras? ¿Por qué?

   _____

   _____

3. Cuando quieres mandar una tarjeta a un amigo, ¿cómo la mandas?

   _____

4. ¿Cómo te comunicas con tus amigos durante un viaje?

   _____

5. ¿Cómo viaja tu familia si quiere ir de vacaciones?

   _____

6. ¿Cuándo fue la última vez que viajaste con tu familia? ¿Por cuánto tiempo estuvieron de vacaciones?

   _____

   _____

7. ¿Uds. caminaron mucho allí? Si no, ¿cómo pasaron de un lugar a otro?

   _____

8. ¿Cómo es un día normal para ti? ¿En qué es diferente un día de vacaciones?

   _____

   _____

   _____

   _____

Nombre _____    Hora _____

Fecha _____    **WRITING**

## Actividad 13

Your entire Spanish class is coming to your house for a barbecue next weekend. They have asked you to e-mail them and let them know what to bring. Write three complete sentences for each group. Follow the model.

**Modelo**    Celia y Ramón: _Vengan a mi casa a las once. Traigan la mayonesa, la_
_mostaza y la salsa de tomate. No se olviden del cuchillo para servirlos._

**1.** La Srta. Arrojo: _____

_____

_____

_____

**2.** Catrina, Ramona y Carlos: _____

_____

_____

_____

**3.** Luisa y David: _____

_____

_____

_____

**B.** Luisa and David would also like to bring a fruit salad, and have asked you to send them the directions from a cookbook for making one.  Write at least six instructions you would find in the recipe for making a fruit salad. The first one has been done for you.

_Compren las uvas, las manzanas, los plátanos y la piña en el supermercado._

_____

_____

_____

_____

_____

Nombre _____    Hora _____

Fecha _____    **VIDEO**

# Antes de ver el video

## Actividad 1

There are many ways to travel: by plane, boat, bus, train, or car. Mark with an **X** the method of transportation you think would be best for each situation.

| situaciones | avión | barco | autobús | coche | tren |
|---|---|---|---|---|---|
| Tengo sólo una semana de vacaciones y está lejos. | | | | | |
| Estamos planeando ir a Aruba, la isla en el mar Caribe. | | | | | |
| Somos estudiantes y no tenemos mucho dinero. | | | | | |
| Sólo puedo ir al acto de graduación por el fin de semana. | | | | | |
| No me gusta manejar, pero me encanta ver el paisaje. | | | | | |
| Quiero llegar rápido para estar más tiempo con mis primos. | | | | | |
| No está tan lejos, somos muchos y tenemos mucho equipaje. | | | | | |
| Lo más divertido es conocer todas las islas. | | | | | |
| Está lejos pero hay varios pueblos interesantes por el camino. | | | | | |

## ¿Comprendes?

### Actividad 2

Ana is writing to a friend about her upcoming trip. Some of her statements are true and some are false. If the statement is true, write **cierto.** If the statement is false, rewrite it to make it true.

1. Elena y yo estamos planeando un viaje a Rusia para estudiar ruso.

   _____

2. Esta mañana fuimos a la agencia de viajes para comprar el billete.

   _____

3. Un vuelo directo a Londres en avión cuesta cincuenta euros ida y vuelta.

   _____

4. Decidimos viajar en tren y viajamos en el "eurostar" para ir de Barcelona a Londres.

   _____

5. Compramos el billete para estudiantes. La agente nos dijo que muchos niños viajan así.

   _____

6. El viaje dura como catorce horas y quince minutos.

   _____

7. Ya hicimos la reserva.

   _____

### Actividad 3

Answer the following questions based on what happened in the video.

¿Por qué está Ana tan impaciente en la agencia de viajes?

1. _____

2. ¿Para qué van Ana y Elena a Londres y por cuánto tiempo?

   _____

**3.** ¿Cómo quieren ir a Londres? _____

**4.** ¿Qué sugerencia les hace la agente de viajes? _____

_____

**5.** ¿Qué tipo más barato de billete pueden comprar? _____

¿Por qué Elena no está muy segura de viajar en tren?

**6.** _____

¿Cómo deciden finalmente viajar a Londres las muchachas?

**7.** _____

¿Por qué Elena y Ana tienen que regresar a la agencia?

**8.** _____

# Y, ¿qué más?

## Actividad 4

Think about a trip you would like to take one day with a friend or family member. Answer the following questions to help create your itinerary.

¿Qué sitio te gustaría conocer en estas vacaciones?

_____

¿Cómo quieres viajar?

_____

¿Con quién te gustaría ir?

_____

¿Cuánto tiempo tienes para hacer el viaje?

_____

¿Qué documentos necesitas para el viaje?

_____

Nombre _____ Hora _____

Fecha _____ **AUDIO**

## Actividad 5

Listen to the messages recorded by different airlines for customers to listen to as they wait for the next available agent to take their phone call. As you listen to each announcement, identify which picture best matches each taped message. Write the number of the conversation in the blank under the corresponding picture. You will hear each message twice.

_____     _____     _____

_____     _____     _____

## Actividad 6

Several Spanish club members just got back from a summer trip to Europe with their teacher. On the way home from the airport, two girls talk about what happened on the trip and how their classmates acted. As you listen, decide whether the student they are talking about was a **buen(a) turista** or **mal(a) turista** and mark the grid below with your answer. You will hear each conversation twice.

|                | 1 | 2 | 3 | 4 | 5 | 6 |
|----------------|---|---|---|---|---|---|
| **Buen(a) turista** |   |   |   |   |   |   |
| **Mal(a) turista**  |   |   |   |   |   |   |

**Realidades 2**

**Capítulo 8A**

Nombre _____

Hora _____

Fecha _____

**AUDIO**

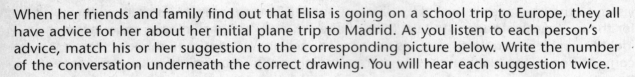

## Actividad 7

When her friends and family find out that Elisa is going on a school trip to Europe, they all have advice for her about her initial plane trip to Madrid. As you listen to each person's advice, match his or her suggestion to the corresponding picture below. Write the number of the conversation underneath the correct drawing. You will hear each suggestion twice.

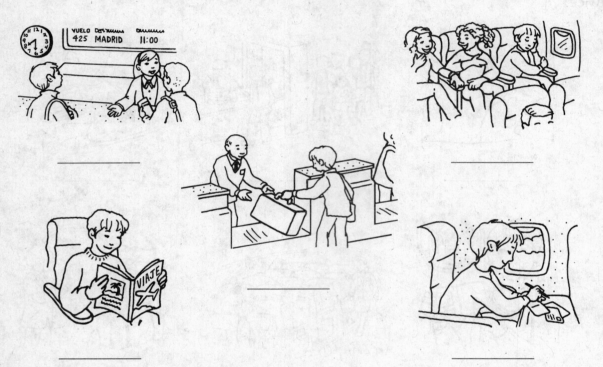

## Actividad 8

Listen to a panel of seasoned travelers and school officials as they give suggestions to students who are taking a trip next month. As you listen to each suggestion, decide whether it is a: **a) sugerencia para planear el viaje; b) sugerencia para el aeropuerto y durante el vuelo; c) sugerencia para cuando viajan por las ciudades que visitan;** or **d) sugerencia sobre qué comprar como recuerdo del viaje.** Write the correct letter in each space below. You will hear each suggestion twice.

1. _____    3. _____    5. _____    7. _____    9. _____

2. _____    4. _____    6. _____    8. _____    10. _____

**Realidades 2**

**Capítulo 8A**

Nombre

Hora

Fecha

**AUDIO**

## Actividad 9

People sometimes encounter difficulties while traveling. As you listen to each of these three people discuss his or her problem, determine what the problem is and circle the appropriate answer. You will hear each discussion twice.

| Viajero(a) | Problema |
|---|---|
| Sr. Machado | **a.** Necesita ir a Chile para una reunión importante por la tarde.<br>**b.** No tiene su pasaporte para pasar por la aduana.<br>**c.** Su vuelo directo a Buenos Aires llega demasiado tarde. |
| Sra. Manizales | **a.** Perdió a su mejor amigo en el aeropuerto.<br>**b.** Olvidó el oso de peluche de su hija en el avión.<br>**c.** Olvidó una maleta en el avión. |
| Luis | **a.** Él es muy impaciente.<br>**b.** Tiene miedo de las inspecciones de seguridad.<br>**c.** Llegó tarde al avión. |

**Realidades 2**

**Capítulo 8A**

Nombre _____

Fecha _____

Hora _____

**WRITING**

## Actividad 10

You are showing your friend Ricardo your pictures from a recent trip to Guatemala. Because Ricardo has never traveled by plane, he is curious about what it was like. Describe your trip to him, using the photos below to help you.

1 _____ .

2. _____ .

3. _____ .

4. _____ .

5. _____ .

6. _____ .

7. _____ .

8. _____ .

**Realidades 2**

**Capítulo 8A**

Nombre _____

Hora _____

Fecha _____

**WRITING**

## Actividad 11

Two new students at your school are asking you how to succeed in Spanish class. Answer their questions below in complete sentences.

BERTO: Nos gustaría saber más de la clase de español. Por ejemplo, ¿cuántas horas recomiendas que nosotros estudiemos todas las noches?

TÚ: _____

_____

TITO: ¿Sugieres que nosotros tomemos la clase del profesor Álvarez?

TÚ: _____

_____

BERTO: ¿El profesor Álvarez permite que los estudiantes usen los libros en los exámenes?

TÚ: _____

_____

TITO: ¿Qué más prefiere él que los estudiantes hagan?

TÚ: _____

_____

BERTO: ¿Qué prohíbe que su clase haga?

TÚ: _____

_____

TITO: Otra pregunta: ¿La escuela insiste en que yo tome tres años de español?

TÚ: _____

_____

BERTO: Muchas gracias por tu ayuda. ¿Tienes más recomendaciones para nosotros?

TÚ: _____

_____

_____

**Realidades 2**

**Capítulo 8A**

Nombre _____

Fecha _____

Hora _____

**WRITING**

## Actividad 12

**A.** Some students and teachers are having an informal discussion in the cafeteria about some issues at school. Combine a subject and verb from **Columna A** with a logical subject and verb from **Columna B** to write complete sentences telling what some of the issues are. You may need to add some information to complete the sentences. Follow the model.

| Columna A | Columna B |
|---|---|
| Nosotros/querer | yo/saber el vocabulario |
| Los profesores/preferir | tú/ser malo |
| El principal/prohibir | los profesores/no dar exámenes |
| La profesora de francés/insistir en | nosotros/ir a clase |
| Yo/recomendar | tú/estar despierto |

**Modelo**  *Nosotros queremos que los profesores no den exámenes los lunes.*

1. _____

2. _____

3. _____

4. _____

**B.** Now, write three recommendations to your own school's administration using the verbs **ser, estar, ir, saber,** or **dar.**

1. _____

_____

2. _____

_____

3. _____

_____

_____

## Actividad 13

Your friend Rosario is coming to visit you from Ecuador next week. She is a bit nervous about traveling by plane alone, so you write her an e-mail reminding her of what to do while traveling. Complete the e-mail below with advice for Rosario.

---

**Fecha:** 9/4/04
**Sujeto:** Algunas recomendaciones
**Recipiente:** rosario@xyz.xyz
**De:** _____
**Mensaje:** Hola, Rosario. No puedo esperar hasta tu llegada.
Antes de ir al aeropuerto, quiero que des el
número de tu vuelo a tus padres.

_____

_____

_____

_____

_____

_____

_____

_____

_____

_____

_____

¡Buena suerte y te veo pronto!

_____

---

Nombre _____  Hora _____

Fecha _____  **VIDEO**

# Antes de ver el video

## Actividad 1

What are the first things you want to do when you arrive in a new city? Make a list of five activities you would do upon arriving in a foreign city. Follow the model.

| Modelo | *Caminar* _____ |

1. _____

2. _____

3. _____

4. _____

5. _____

# ¿Comprendes?

## Actividad 2

Read each of the following descriptions and decide whether it describes Ignacio, Javier, or both (**los dos**). Circle the correct answer for each.

1. Tiene un partido de fútbol mañana.  **Ignacio  Javier  Los dos**

2. Quiere comprar alguna artesanía.  **Ignacio  Javier  Los dos**

3. Compra una guía.  **Ignacio  Javier  Los dos**

4. Es la primera vez que visita Toledo sin sus padres.  **Ignacio  Javier  Los dos**

5. Quiere regatear por la espada (*sword*).  **Ignacio  Javier  Los dos**

6. Le gusta la ciudad de Toledo.  **Ignacio  Javier  Los dos**

7. Compra unas tarjetas postales.  **Ignacio  Javier  Los dos**

8. Dice que está cansado.  **Ignacio  Javier  Los dos**

Nombre _____ Hora _____

Fecha _____

**VIDEO**

## Actividad 3

Next to each video scene, write a sentence describing what was happening at that moment in the video. Follow the model.

**Modelo**    *Ignacio y Javier van a dejar sus cosas en el hotel.* _____

1. _____

   _____

2. _____

   _____

3. _____

   _____

4. _____

   _____

5. _____

   _____

6. _____

   _____

7. _____

   _____

**Realidades 2**

**Capítulo 8B**

Nombre _____

Hora _____

Fecha _____

**VIDEO**

# Y, ¿qué más?

## Actividad 4

Your friend is going on her first plane trip out of the country. Write five sentences of advice for her. Follow the model.

**Modelo**  *Te aconsejo que tengas siempre buenos modales con la gente.*

_____

_____

_____

_____

_____

_____

_____

_____

**Realidades 2**

**Capítulo 8B**

Nombre _____

Fecha _____

Hora _____

**AUDIO**

## Actividad 5

Listen as several tourists in Spain call the front desk of the hotel for assistance. Then, write the number of the phone call under the corresponding picture. You will hear each phone call twice.

_____

_____

_____

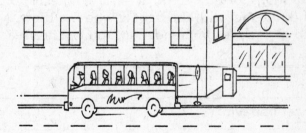

_____

_____

**Realidades** ❷

**Capítulo 8B**

Nombre _____

Hora _____

Fecha _____

**AUDIO**

## Actividad 6

A student tour group is on the train to begin a two-day tour of the historic town of Toledo, Spain. Eager to use the Spanish they have learned, they talk to some of the Spanish-speaking passengers on the train. As you listen to each conversation, place a check mark under the picture of the place they are talking about in the grid below. You will hear each conversation twice.

|   |   |   |   |   |
|---|---|---|---|---|
| 1 |   |   |   |   |
| 2 |   |   |   |   |
| 3 |   |   |   |   |
| 4 |   |   |   |   |
| 5 |   |   |   |   |

## Actividad 7

Although Sra. Milano wants her Spanish students to enjoy their first trip to Spain, she also wants to be sure that they behave appropriately while they are there. Listen as she gives them advice at their last meeting before they leave on their trip. Categorize her advice as suggestions for how to: a) act in the hotel; b) dress while touring; c) stay safe on the trip; and d) interact with the people who live there. Mark with an X the appropriate box as you listen to each recommendation. You will hear each recommendation twice.

|                          | 1 | 2 | 3 | 4 | 5 | 6 | 7 |
|--------------------------|---|---|---|---|---|---|---|
| **Hotel behavior**       |   |   |   |   |   |   |   |
| **Appropriate dress**    |   |   |   |   |   |   |   |
| **Safety**               |   |   |   |   |   |   |   |
| **Interacting with people** |   |   |   |   |   |   |   |

Nombre _____

Hora _____

Fecha _____

**AUDIO**

## Actividad 8

A few graduating seniors have recorded messages with advice for the underclassmen in their schools. Match each senior with the topics of his or her advice by placing a check mark in the corresponding box. You will hear each message twice.

|  | pedir ayuda | sentirse contento | reírse | recordar a los amigos | no perder tiempo (*waste time*) | divertirse | no mentir | seguir sus sueños |
|---|---|---|---|---|---|---|---|---|
| Isabel |  |  |  |  |  |  |  |  |
| Jorge |  |  |  |  |  |  |  |  |
| Lisa |  |  |  |  |  |  |  |  |
| Beto |  |  |  |  |  |  |  |  |

## Actividad 9

Listen as teenagers use their international calling cards to talk to their parents while they travel in Spain. Based on what each says, match a picture below to the main idea of his or her conversation. You will hear each conversation twice.

_____    _____

_____    _____

## Actividad 10

You are working at a travel agency answering e-mails from travelers who have questions. Read their questions below and answer them in complete sentences.

1. Mi esposo y yo queremos hacer una reservación en un hotel. ¿Qué tipo de habitación debemos conseguir?

   _____

2. ¿Cómo es un buen turista? ¿Qué cosa no hace?

   _____

   _____

3. ¿Qué actividades puedo hacer en el lago Ontario?

   _____

   _____

4. Voy a Madrid y no sé qué lugares debo visitar. ¿Dónde busco esta información?

   _____

   _____

5. En los mercados de México, ¿debemos aceptar el precio que el vendedor nos dice?

   _____

6. ¿A quiénes les doy una propina en los Estados Unidos?

   _____

   _____

7. Cuando llego al hotel, ¿adónde voy?

   _____

8. ¿Adónde voy para cambiar dinero al llegar a Argentina?

   _____

**Realidades 2**

**Capítulo 8B**

Nombre _____

Fecha _____

Hora _____

**WRITING**

## Actividad 11

Your school has handed out a survey to students in order find out their opinions on different topics related to school life. Write two opinions for each category below, using complete sentences. The first one has been done for you.

1. la comida

   *Es importante que sirvan pizza todos los días.*

   *Quiero que preparen galletas de chocolate.*

2. los autobuses

   _____

   _____

3. las horas de la escuela

   _____

   _____

4. las clases

   _____

   _____

5. los deportes

   _____

   _____

6. los profesores

   _____

   _____

7. los estudiantes

   _____

   _____

**Realidades 2**

**Capítulo 8B**

Nombre _____

Hora _____

Fecha _____

**WRITING**

## Actividad 12

You are helping your Health teacher make fliers for Health Awareness Week. Using the phrases below, write six recommendations on the flier to the people indicated in the parentheses. Then, write six recommendations about what they should avoid. Use complete sentences. The first one has been done for you.

jugar a los deportes (los jóvenes)

perder peso (los estadounidenses)

acostarse temprano (tú)

comenzar un programa de ejercicio (los estudiantes)

seguir las sugerencias del médico (nosotros)

pedir comida saludable (la gente)

~~dormir ocho horas (nosotros)~~

---

### LA SEMANA DE LA SALUD

- *Nos recomienda que durmamos ocho horas cada noche.*

  *Es mejor que no comamos muchas galletas.*

- _____

  _____

- _____

  _____

- _____

  _____

- _____

  _____

- _____

  _____

- _____

  _____

**Realidades 2**

**Capítulo 8B**

Nombre _____

Fecha _____

Hora _____

**WRITING**

## Actividad 13

Your younger brother and sister are going on a trip to Spain with their class and have asked you to help them get ready.

**A.** First, organize your thoughts by writing appropriate responses to their questions below.

¿Qué debemos traer al aeropuerto?

_____    _____

_____    _____

_____    _____

¿Qué/A quiénes vamos a encontrar en el aeropuerto?

_____    _____

_____    _____

_____    _____

**B.** Now, give your siblings advice about their trip using the ideas you wrote above. Follow the model.

| Modelo |  A tu hermano:

*Es necesario que traigas tu carnet de identificación al aeropuerto.*

A tu hermana:

_____

_____

_____

_____

A los dos:

_____

_____

_____

_____

Nombre _____

Hora _____

Fecha _____

**VIDEO**

# Antes de ver el video

## Actividad 1

There are many different professions and careers you might choose to pursue. In the first column below, write five professions or careers that interest you. In the second column, write something with which each career or profession is associated. The first one is done for you.

**Carrera o profesión**

*Profesor(a)* _____

_____

_____

_____

_____

**Cosas**

*la educación* _____

_____

_____

_____

_____

# ¿Comprendes?

## Actividad 2

Each of the following sentences is false. Rewrite each one to make it true.

1. Angélica prefiere el mundo de las artes.

_____

2. Pedro dijo: "A mí me gusta todo tipo de arte. Y me encanta correr."

_____

_____

3. Pedro podría ser médico; le gusta mucho escribir.

_____

_____

**Realidades 2**

**Capítulo 9A**

Nombre _____

Hora _____

Fecha _____

VIDEO

Esteban quiere estudiar para ingeniero o contador. Le gustan las profesiones técnicas.

**4.** _____

_____

Esteban pide la dirección electrónica de Pedro.

_____

**5.** _____

## Actividad 3

Answer each of the following questions in complete sentences based on what you saw in the video.

**1.** ¿Por qué quieren ir los amigos al colegio un domingo?

_____

**2.** ¿Qué dice Angélica cuando ve el dibujo de Pedro?

_____

**3.** ¿Cómo prefiere Angélica ganarse la vida algún día?

_____

**4.** ¿Cómo prefiere Esteban ganarse la vida algún día?

_____

**5.** ¿Cuándo van a graduarse los amigos?

_____

**6.** ¿Por qué dice Pedro: "Gracias, es un momento muy importante para mí"?

_____

Nombre _____    Hora _____

Fecha _____    **VIDEO**

# Y, ¿qué más?

## Actividad 4

The friends from the video seem to know what they want to be when they are older. Think about the five professions you wrote about in **Actividad 1** and how you can work towards achieving each goal. Use the model to guide you.

| Modelo | *Para ser profesora yo necesito ir a la universidad y estudiar educación. También necesito aprender a enseñar la clase.* |

1. _____
_____
_____

2. _____
_____
_____

3. _____
_____
_____

4. _____
_____
_____

5. _____
_____
_____

**Realidades** 2

**Capítulo 9A**

Nombre _____

Fecha _____

Hora _____

**AUDIO**

## Actividad 5

Listen to the following students describe their interests and talents, then match each one up with his or her ideal career by writing the number of the statement under the corresponding picture. You will hear each statement twice.

_____

_____

_____

_____

_____

_____

**AUDIO**

## Actividad 6

Listen to the latest listings that were recently posted on a job hotline. Match the job qualifications with each of the pictures below by writing the number of each conversation underneath the corresponding picture. You will hear each listing twice.

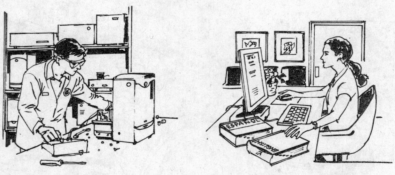

## Actividad 7

Listen as friends get together and talk about what they would like to do as a career in the future. What seems to motivate each of them the most? Is it: a) the imagined salary; b) the possibility of fame; or c) the possible benefit of his or her work to society? Listen to each person and place an X in the corresponding box in the grid. You will hear each conversation twice.

| | 1 | 2 | 3 | 4 | 5 | 6 | 7 |
|---|---|---|---|---|---|---|---|
| ¿El salario? | | | | | | | |
| ¿La fama? | | | | | | | |
| ¿Los beneficios a la sociedad? | | | | | | | |

## Actividad 8

The first day on the job can be a challenge for anyone. Listen as these people are shown around their new offices. As you listen to each conversation, determine what kind of job each person has. In the blanks provided, write the letter of the picture that corresponds to each conversation. You will hear each conversation twice.

A          B          C

D          E          F

1. _____  2. _____  3. _____  4. _____  5. _____  6. _____

## Actividad 9

There are advantages and disadvantages to choosing a career in art. As you listen to each statement, check off whether it describes an advantage (**ventaja**) or disadvantage (**desventaja**) of being in the art industry. You will hear each statement twice.

|  | 1 | 2 | 3 | 4 | 5 | 6 | 7 | 8 | 9 | 10 |
|---|---|---|---|---|---|---|---|---|---|---|
| **Ventaja** | | | | | | | | | | |
| **Desventaja** | | | | | | | | | | |

**Realidades 2**

**Capítulo 9A**

Nombre _____

Hora _____

Fecha _____

WRITING

## Actividad 10

Your friend Carolina is visiting from Ecuador, and you have taken her to your neighborhood's annual summer party. Using the picture below, write complete sentences to tell her what each person at the party does for a living and what the job entails. Follow the model.

| Modelo | *Ella es diseñadora. Diseña y dibuja ropa de hombres y mujeres.* |

A. _____

B. _____

C. _____

D. _____

E. _____

F. _____

G. _____

H. _____

I. _____

J. _____

**Realidades 2**

**Capítulo 9A**

Nombre _____

Hora _____

Fecha _____

**WRITING**

## Actividad 11

You and your friends are making predictions about what life will be like in the year 2100. Use your imagination to write complete sentences about the topics listed below. Follow the model.

**Modelo**   los niños   *A todos los niños les encantará ir a la escuela.* _____

1. los coches _____

   _____

2. la comida _____

   _____

3. los colegios _____

   _____

4. las casas _____

   _____

5. yo _____

   _____

6. nosotros _____

   _____

7. nuestro planeta _____

   _____

8. los Estados Unidos _____

   _____

9. mi familia _____

   _____

10. la ciudad de Nueva York _____

   _____

## Actividad 12

Juanito is running for class president. Help him write his campaign promises about each topic by using the following verbs: **hacer, poder, saber, tener,** and **haber.** You may use each verb twice. Follow the model.

**Modelo** La escuela *tendrá tres cafeterías.* _____

1. Yo _____.

_____

2. Los profesores _____.

_____

3. El baile de la escuela _____.

_____

4. Los estudiantes _____.

_____

5. Mis mejores amigos y yo _____.

_____

6. El día escolar _____.

_____

7. La administración _____.

_____

8. Nosotros _____.

_____

9. La cafetería _____.

_____

10. Los deportes _____.

_____

**Realidades 2**

**Capítulo 9A**

Nombre _____

Hora _____

Fecha _____

**WRITING**

## Actividad 13

You are playing the fortune-teller at your school's winter carnival. Some of your friends want to find out what is going to happen to them in the future. Write at least three predictions for each of the people listed below. The first one has been started for you.

1. Nombre de un(a) amigo(a) _____

   Predicciones:

   *Mi amigo tendrá una casa grande.* _____

   _____

   _____

   _____

2. Nombre de dos amigos(as): _____ y _____

   Predicciones:

   _____

   _____

   _____

   _____

3. (Yo) Predicciones:

   _____

   _____

   _____

   _____

4. (Nosotros) Predicciones:

   _____

   _____

   _____

   _____

**Realidades 2**

**Capítulo 9B**

Nombre _____

Hora _____

Fecha _____

**VIDEO**

# Antes de ver el video

## Actividad 1

Make a list of five things that can affect the environment or the Earth in general. One has been done for you.

1. _____ *guerra* _____

2. _____

3. _____

4. _____

5. _____

# ¿Comprendes?

## Actividad 2

Answer the following questions in order to better understand what happened in the video.

1. Pedro está en casa de Esteban. ¿Qué pasa?

_____

2. ¿Qué piensa Pedro?

_____

3. Ellos tienen mucho calor. ¿Adónde deciden ir y por qué?

_____

**Realidades 2**

**Capítulo 9B**

Nombre _____

Hora _____

Fecha _____

**VIDEO**

**4.** ¿De qué hablan Esteban y Pedro cuando van caminando al cine?

_____

**5.** ¿A quién llama Esteban por el teléfono celular y para qué?

_____

## Actividad 3

Pedro and Esteban are talking about the good and bad effects things we use every day have on the environment. Write what each boy says about the following things.

Modelo **bicicleta**

Pedro: *reduce la contaminación y ahorra dinero*

Esteban: *el coche es más cómodo y más rápido*

1. **aire acondicionado solar**

Pedro: _____

Esteban: _____

2. **aire acondicionado**

Pedro: _____

Esteban: _____

3. **coche**

Pedro: _____

Esteban: _____

4. **autobús**

Pedro: _____

Esteban: _____

Nombre _____  Hora _____

Fecha _____

**VIDEO**

## Actividad 4

Pedro has some good ideas about how to protect and preserve the environment but he cannot convince Esteban. Think about one way to protect and preserve the environment. Then, write three complete sentences to tell why your idea is important.

1. _____

_____

2. _____

_____

3. _____

_____

**Realidades 2**

**Capítulo 9B**

Nombre _____

Fecha _____

Hora _____

**AUDIO**

## Actividad 5

Listen to the following people talk about the future. As you hear each statement, determine whether the speaker is an optimist or a pessimist and place a check mark in the corresponding box in the grid. You will hear each statement twice.

|            | 1 | 2 | 3 | 4 | 5 | 6 | 7 | 8 |
|------------|---|---|---|---|---|---|---|---|
| **Optimista** |   |   |   |   |   |   |   |   |
| **Pesimista** |   |   |   |   |   |   |   |   |

## Actividad 6

Listen as students in Sr. Naranjo's science class make predictions about the year 2020. As you hear each one, mark the number of the description underneath the picture it describes. Then, mark an X in the grid below to tell whether you agree with the prediction or doubt it will come true. Be prepared to tell why you answered the way you did. You will hear each prediction twice.

_____   _____   _____   _____

|                   | 1 | 2 | 3 | 4 | 5 | 6 | 7 |
|-------------------|---|---|---|---|---|---|---|
| **Lo dudo**        |   |   |   |   |   |   |   |
| **Estoy de acuerdo** |   |   |   |   |   |   |   |

**Realidades 2**

**Capítulo 9B**

Nombre _____

Hora _____

Fecha _____

**AUDIO**

## Actividad 7

Listen as Julia and Elena plan Julia's campaign for class president. Some of the campaign promises they come up with are a) silly and not possible, while others are b) serious and possible. As you listen to each idea, write **a** or **b** in the blanks provided. You will hear each statement twice.

1. _____  2. _____  3. _____  4. _____  5. _____  6. _____  7. _____  8. _____

## Actividad 8

The debate coach is observing a mock debate in order to determine whom she will select as partners (**compañeros**) for an upcoming debate on "**El futuro para nosotros.**" Listen as the debaters answer the coach's questions. Fill in the chart below by circling each debater's opinion on the three issues. Which two people share the most opinions? You will hear each conversation twice.

|  | Las escuelas sin profesores | La paz mundial (*world peace*) | Vivir en la Luna |
|---|---|---|---|
| **Ramón** | Es posible  Es imposible | Es posible  Es imposible | Es posible  Es imposible |
| **Sandra** | Es posible  Es imposible | Es posible  Es imposible | Es posible  Es imposible |
| **Lucas** | Es posible  Es imposible | Es posible  Es imposible | Es posible  Es imposible |

¿Quiénes deben ser compañeros? _____

## Actividad 9

Listen to this class discussion about the problems in the world and solutions for a better world in the future. As you hear each comment, decide if the person is describing a problem or offering a solution. Place a check mark in the appropriate column in the grid below. You will hear each comment twice.

|  | 1 | 2 | 3 | 4 | 5 | 6 | 7 | 8 |
|---|---|---|---|---|---|---|---|---|
| **Problema** |  |  |  |  |  |  |  |  |
| **Solución** |  |  |  |  |  |  |  |  |

Nombre _____     Hora _____

Fecha _____

**WRITING**

## Actividad 10

Look at the drawings below of environmental problems and their solutions. Describe how each one affects the environment. Write two complete sentences for each. Follow the model.

**Modelo**    *Hay mucho humo que causa la contaminación del aire.*
*Es un problema grave para el pueblo.*

1. _____

_____

_____

2. _____

_____

_____

3. _____

_____

_____

4. _____

_____

_____

5. _____

_____

_____

6. _____

_____

**Realidades 2**

**Capítulo 9B**

Nombre _____

Hora _____

Fecha _____

**WRITING**

## Actividad 11

The Valencia family is making plans to move to a new house. Look at the pictures below and tell what each person is planning, using the future tense of the verbs provided.

1.    yo (poner)

_____.

2.    Marisa (querer)

_____.

3.    nosotros (salir)

_____.

4.    mis amigos (venir)

_____.

5.    yo (hacer)

_____.

6.    tú (decir)

_____.

Nombre _____ Hora _____

Fecha _____ **WRITING**

## Actividad 12

Humberto is listening to the president's speech on the radio and is skeptical about what he hears. Read the excerpts below from the speech and write Humberto's reactions using phrases to express doubt. The first one has been done for you.

Los Estados Unidos deben ahorrar sus recursos naturales. Tendremos que conservar energía y reciclar para poder disfrutar una buena vida. Yo quiero reducir la contaminación del medio ambiente en los años que vienen...

También, quiero hacer planes para resolver nuestros conflictos internacionales. No podemos vivir si seguimos luchando entre países...

... Tenemos un problema con la economía. Les sugiero que los mejores economistas trabajen para mejorarla... Todos tienen que juntarse para proteger la Tierra... Mi plan puede funcionar si todos trabajamos juntos.

1. *Dudo que conservemos energía.* _____

2. _____

3. _____

4. _____

5. _____

6. _____

7. _____

8. _____

**WRITING**

## Actividad 13

You and your friends are proposing a plan to help preserve the environment, starting right in your own school.

**A.** Write a proposal to your school to launch your plan by listing five things you, your friends, and your school can do to make a difference. Use the future tense of some of the following verbs: **haber, hacer, poner, saber, decir, tener, venir, querer.** The first one has been done for you.

Tenemos que proteger nuestra Tierra. Por eso, nosotros haremos muchos cambios en nuestros hábitos:

- *Reciclaremos las latas y las botellas.* _____

- _____

- _____

- _____

- _____

- _____

**B.** Next, persuade the administration to accept your proposal by describing the environmental consequences of your plan. The description has been started for you.

*Si seguimos este plan, veremos muchos cambios importantes. Es seguro que la*

*Tierra mejorará. Dudamos que la destrucción continúe.* _____

_____

_____

_____

_____

_____

# Song Lyrics

These are the lyrics for the songs that appear on the Canciones CD.

## Track 01
### SOÑANDO CON PUERTO RICO

Si por casualidad duermes y sueñas
que te acaricia la brisa,
y sueñas que el rocío mañanero
besa tiernamente tu mejilla,
y el aroma del café te hace cosquillas,
seguro sueñas que estás en Puerto Rico.

Si por casualidad duermo y notas
que una lágrima me brota,
seguramente es que yo sueño que camino
por las calles de mi pueblo,
y en el ventorillo aquel de mis recuerdos,
reviví el ayer quizás llorando.

Yo, yo no puedo ocultar el orgullo que siento
de ser puertorriqueña
y que mi pensamiento por do'quiera que voy
se arrulla a aquella islita;
por do'quiera que voy
a la tierra bendita
mi pensamiento vuela.

Si por casualidad duermo y notas
que una lágrima me brota. . .
(se repite)

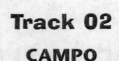

# Track 02

## CAMPO

Campo, yo vivo triste
cada día sufriendo más.
¡Ay, Dios! ¿qué será de mí?
Si no bailo esa bomba,
me voy a morir.

Campo, yo vivo triste
cada día sufriendo más.
¡Ay, Dios! ¿qué será de mí?
Si no bailo esa bomba,
me voy a morir.

Oye, Campito, yo vivo triste,
cada día sufriendo más.
¡Ay, Dios! ¿qué será de mí?
Si no bailo esa bomba,
me voy a morir.

Campo, campo yo vivo triste
cada día sufriendo más.
¡Ay, Dios! ¿qué será de mí?
Si no bailo esa bomba,
me voy a morir.

Sí, milonga, le digo a Maicolina,
Maicolina, échate pa' aquí.
¡Yo quiero bailar la bomba!
Si no la bailo, me voy a morir.
¡Campo, Campo!

Campo, yo vivo triste
cada día sufriendo más.
¡Ay, Dios! ¿qué será de mí?
Si no bailo esa bomba,
me voy a morir.

Oye, Campita, yo vivo triste,
cada día yo sufro más.
¡Ay, Dios! ¿qué será de mí?
Si no bailo esa bomba,
me voy a morir.
¡Campo, Campo!

Campo, yo vivo triste
cada día sufriendo más.
¡Ay, Dios! ¿qué será de mí?
Si no bailo esa bomba,
me voy a morir.

# Track 03

## GUANTANAMERA

Guantanamera, guajira Guantanamera
Guantanamera, guajira Guantanamera
Guantanamera, guajira Guantanamera
Guantanamera, guajira Guantanamera

Yo soy un hombre sincero
de donde crece la palma.
Yo soy un hombre sincero
de donde crece la palma.
Y antes de morirme quiero
Echar los versos del alma.

Guantanamera, guajira Guantanamera
Guantanamera, guajira Guantanamera

Mi verso es de un verde claro
y de un carmín encendido.
Mi verso es de un verde claro
y de un carmín encendido.
Mi verso es un ciervo herido
que busca en el monte amparo.

Guantanamera, guajira Guantanamera
Guantanamera, guajira Guantanamera
Guantanamera, guajira Guantanamera
Guantanamera, guajira Guantanamera

Con los pobres de mi tierra
quiero yo mi suerte echar.
Con los pobres de mi tierra
quiero yo mi suerte echar.
El arroyo de la sierra
me complace más que el mar.

Guantanamera, guajira Guantanamera
Guantanamera, guajira Guantanamera
Guantanamera, guajira Guantanamera
Guantanamera, guajira Guantanamera

# Track 04

## EN MI VIEJO SAN JUAN

En mi viejo San Juan cuántos sueños
forjé
en mis años de infancia.
Mi primera ilusión y mis cuitas
de amor
son recuerdos del alma.
Una tarde partí
hacia extraña nación
pues lo quiso el destino.
Pero mi corazón se quedó frente al
mar
en mi viejo San Juan.

(Coro)  Adiós..., Borinquen querida.
Adiós, mi diosa del mar.
Me voy,

Pero un día volveré
a buscar mi querer, a soñar otra vez
en mi viejo San Juan.
Pero el tiempo pasó y el destino
burló
mi terrible nostalgia.
Y no pude volver al San Juan que
yo amé
pedacito de patria.
Mi cabello blanqueó, ya mi vida
se va
Ya la muerte me llama
Y no puedo morir alejada de ti
Puerto Rico del alma.

(Coro)

# Track 05

## CANCIÓN CON TODOS

Salgo a caminar
por la cintura cósmica del Sur,
piso en la región
más vegetal del viento y de la luz;
siento al caminar
toda la piel de América en mi piel
y anda en mi sangre un río
que libera en mi voz su caudal.

Sol de alto Perú,
rostro Bolivia, estaño y soledad;
un verde Brasil,
besa mi Chile cobre y mineral.
Subo desde el sur,
hacia la entraña América y total,
pura raíz y un grito
destinado a crecer y a estallar.

Todas las voces, todas;
todas las manos, todas;
toda la sangre puede
ser canción en el viento
Canta conmigo, canta, latinoamericano
libera tu esperanza
con un grito en la voz.

## Track 06

### CUENTO DEL MUNDO

Yo le contaba del mundo
del mundo y su alrededor,
de su misterio profundo, de su forma y su
extensión,
de su misterio profundo, de su forma y su
extensión.

De sus llanuras inmensas,
de su aurora de arrebol,
de sus aves, de sus fieras, de su Luna y de
su sol,
de sus aves, de sus fieras, de su Luna y de
su sol.

¿De qué color es el mundo?
que la sombra pregunta.
"Justo del color que quiera pintarle tu
corazón."
"Justo del color que quiera pintarle tu
corazón."

Yo le contaba del mundo,
de su sentido y razón,
de lo que parece absurdo y no tiene
explicación,
de lo que parece absurdo y no tiene
explicación.

De su calor, de su frío,
de su silencio y su voz,
de su camino infinito, de su dicha y su dolor,
de su camino infinito, de su dicha y su dolor.

¿De qué color es el mundo?
que la sombra pregunta.
"Justo del color que quiera pintarle tu
corazón."

## Track 07

### LA MEDIA VUELTA

Te vas porque yo quiero que te vayas.
A la hora que yo quiero te detengo.
Yo sé que tu cariño me hace falta
aunque quieras o no, yo soy tu dueña.

Yo quiero que te vayas por el mundo
y quiero que conozcas mucha gente.
Yo quiero que te besen otros labios
para que me compares hoy como
siempre.

Si encuentras un amor que te
comprenda
y sientas que te quiere más que nadie,
entonces yo daré la media vuelta
y me iré con el sol cuando muera la
tarde,
Entonces yo daré la media vuelta
y me iré con el sol cuando muera la
tarde.

# Track 08

## CANCIÓN MIXTECA

¡Qué lejos estoy del suelo donde he nacido!
¡Qué inmensa nostalgia invade mi
pensamiento!
Y al verme tan solo y triste, cual hoja al
viento,
quisiera llorar, quisiera morir de
sentimiento.

¡Oh tierra del sol suspiro por verte!
Ahora qué lejos yo vivo sin luz, sin amor.
Y al verme tan solo y triste, cual hoja al
viento,
quisiera llorar, quisiera morir de
sentimiento.

¡Oh tierra del sol suspiro por verte!
Ahora qué lejos yo vivo sin luz, sin amor.
Y al verme tan solo y triste, cual hoja al
viento,
quisiera llorar, quisiera morir de
sentimiento.

# Track 09

## SÓLO LE PIDO A DIOS

Sólo le pido a Dios que el dolor no me sea
indiferente,
que la reseca muerte no me encuentre
vacía y sola sin haber hecho lo suficiente.

Sólo le pido a Dios que lo injusto no me sea
indiferente,
que no me abofeteen la otra mejilla
después de que una garra me arañó esa
suerte.

Sólo le pido a Dios que la guerra no me sea
indiferente.
Es un monstruo grande y pisa fuerte
toda la pobre inocencia de la gente.

Sólo le pido a Dios que el engaño no me sea
indiferente;
si un traidor puede más que unos cuantos,
que esos cuantos no lo olviden fácilmente.

Sólo le pido a Dios que el futuro no me sea
indiferente.
Desahuciado está el que tiene que marchar
a vivir a una cultura diferente.

Sólo le pido a Dios, sólo a Dios
que la guerra, que la guerra no me sea
indiferente.
Sólo a Dios
Es un monstruo grande y pisa fuerte
toda la pobre inocencia de la gente.

Es un monstruo grande y pisa fuerte
toda la pobre inocencia de la gente.

# Track 10

## VERDE LUZ

Verde luz de monte y mar,
isla virgen de coral,
si me ausento de tus playas rumorosas,
si me alejo de tus palmas silenciosas,
quiero volver, quiero volver.

A sentir la tibia arena,
a dormirme en tus riberas,
isla mía, flor cautiva,
para ti quiero tener.

Libre tu cielo, sola tu estrella, isla doncella
quiero tener
Verde luz de monte y mar.

# Track 11

## MI CUATRITO

Yo tengo un cuatrito que canta clarito,
Como ruiseñores que cantan muy bien.
Lo pulso y responde con voz melodiosa,
Me canta las cosas de mi Borinquen.

A tiempo remoto lo llevo conmigo
y es muy buen testigo de mis amoríos,
Con él he cantado a seres queridos,
y me ha divertido en horas de hastío.

Con él he gozado, con él he sufrido.
Con él he pasado miles sinsabores,
oh dulce cuatrito, fiel compañerito,
testigo de todos mis viejos amores.

Oh dulce cuatrito, cántale a mi amada,
la fiera dorada de mi corazón.
Contigo y con ella viviré la vida,
hasta la partida a la eterna mansión.

## Track 12

### A SAN FERMÍN PEDIMOS

A San Fermín pedimos
por ser nuestro patrón,
que nos proteja en el encierro
y que nos dé su bendición.

## Track 13

### Y VOLVER, VOLVER

Ese amor apasionado
anda todo alborotado
por volver.
Voy camino a la locura,
y aunque todo me tortura,
sé querer.

Nos dejamos tanto tiempo,
pero me llegó el momento de perder.
Y tú tenías mucha razón,
le hago caso al corazón
y me muero por volver.

Y volver, volver, volver
a tus brazos otra vez.
Llegaré hasta donde estés.
Yo sé perder, yo sé perder,
quiero volver, volver, volver.